The Shaman Sorceress

The Shaman Sorceress

KIM DONG-NI

Translated by

HYUN SONG SHIN and EUGENE CHUNG

KEGAN PAUL INTERNATIONAL
London and New York

First published in 1989 by Kegan Paul International Limited
PO Box 256, London WC1B 3SW

Distributed by
International Thomson Publishing Services Ltd
North Way, Andover, Hants SP10 5BE

Routledge, Chapman and Hall Inc
29 West 35th Street
New York, NY 10001
USA

The Canterbury Press Pty Ltd
Unit 2, 71 Rushdale Street
Scoresby, Victoria 3179
Australia

Set in Times
by Columns of Reading
and printed in Great Britain
by T. J. Press

Korean Culture Series: edited by Chung Chang-Wha

ISBN 07103 0280 0

Chapter One
THE HOUSE OF
THE SORCERESS

Even as Eulhwa came back with the water from the well at the shrine Wolhie was still fast asleep. The well at the shrine, deep and agèd, was a good four hundred metres' walk from her house and was sited next to the sacred tree dedicated to the guardian spirit of the village.

Eulhwa had made a habit of going to the well every morning – before anyone else, and would fill her small earthenware jar to the brim and then would wash her face before returning home.

There was the exceptional taste of the deep water but this wasn't the only reason Eulhwa made the return journey of nearly one kilometre every morning. The main reason lay somewhere else, that, it was unthinkable for anyone to draw water from someone else's well before the owner himself did. As for washing oneself there, it would be an unspeakable breach of communal ethics.

Eulhwa put down the pail on the kitchen range and carefully poured out a small bowlful of water and placing it on a small black table which had been wiped meticulously clean, and carrying it with both hands, went into the room.

This sanctum Eulhwa called her home had a large wooden-floored room to the East, another smaller 'Ondol'[1] room next to it, and to the West was this spacious kitchen.

The very day she had moved into the house she had erected an altar in the large wooden-floored room, on which she kept

1

the effigy of her guardian goddess, the tutelary bronze mirror and other sacred objects. Since then she had acquired numerous shamanistic paintings and they now cluttered all four walls. Apart from these, there were the sundry musical instruments for the rites, the ritual costume and equipment, all set neatly in their proper places.

However, soon after moving in, she found it too much of a nuisance for her to go to the East room, whether to perform the daily propitiation rituals or the even more frequent incantations, and so another, smaller altar was prepared in one corner of the stone-floored Ondol room where the sorceress and her daughter slept. To this altar, she was obliged to move the effigy of her guardian spirit and the bronze mirror.

When Eulhwa came into the room with the small bowl of water, Wolhie was still sleeping as if it was in the middle of the night. Despite the blackish swarm of flies on the nose and cheek of her snow-white face, she was thus sound asleep.

But as if she was not aware of her daughter's presence, Eulhwa placed the bowl of water on the altar, lifted herself up slowly and began her incantation rubbing the palms of her hands together.

'Oh Heavenly spirit, our spirit, great spirit, who gives us luck, who gives us a place to rest, who chases away misfortune, please look kindly upon this mother and daughter, keep from harm our lives as delicate as thread! And Heavenly spirit, great spirit, that goblin with the large horns which visited me last night in my dream, wherever it came from and however it came, it is still circling this area. Please chase it away with one reproof and never let it even set foot in this house! Oh Heavenly spirit, our spirit, to you I pray. Not to let the horned goblin ever to come near this house, never let it near this mother and her daughter. Chase it ten leagues away, a hundred leagues away, . . .'

It was a husky, one could almost say 'sticky' voice. She lifted her hands above her head and buckled her well formed, handsome waist and made three deep bows. Through the long slender fingers of her hands as she lifted them for each bow, there glistened the dark flame of the black eyes.

Wolhie was still asleep and the light regular rhythm of her breathing could be heard. But as if she didn't mind at all, Eulhwa, wearing a warm smile on the bluish face of hers,

2

chased the flies with one swish of her *chima* (long skirt) and left the room. It was Eulwha's policy never to rouse her daughter from her sleep until she woke of her own accord.

Coming out into the kitchen, Eulhwa laid the breakfast table. But laying the table was an easy job for it was the same dish of *kimchi* and a little soy sauce, together with three bowls of rice and two of water. This was all, and had been so, every day.

It was when the cooked rice was being scooped into the bowls that Wolhie woke up. The only time she would venture out of the room throughout the whole day was when she came out into the yard to wash. And equally regularly, she would visit the toilet before breakfast, almost having to plough her way through the dense growth of weeds. While Wolhie was thus away, Eulhwa would pour some water into the earthen wash basin and place it in the yard. Then Wolhie would come and wash her face and toss the water over the weeds. And invariably she would go into the room without a word of greeting. There were no greetings, even on their first meeting every morning.

When Eulhwa entered with the breakfast table, Wolhie was looking at herself in the small hand mirror in the middle of the room. Apart from painting, the only thing with which Wolhie occupied herself was this, almost childish game of seeing her own image in the hand mirror.

Eulhwa stood there still holding the table and simply stared down at her daughter without telling her to move. Her intoxicated gaze and the spellbound smile came whenever she looked at her daughter. To her, Wolhie's face, neck, shoulders, waist, legs, in fact her appearance as a whole could not be more exquisitely beautiful. She even sensed something sacred and sublime.

As Wolhie put down the mirror and got herself out of the way, Eulhwa recovered her senses, and placed the table in the middle of the room. She now set the first bowl of rice on the altar. This rite was simple to the extreme. There were no incantations or prayers as with the serving of the bowl of water.

'Today's breakfast will be very tasty,' said Eulhwa. The truth was that this breakfast was no different from the others. After all, it was the product of the same water, same rice, the

3

same firewood, and the same hand which cooked it. But Eulhwa would often say such things. Perhaps it was some strange intuition on her part or it was simply to whet the appetite of the listener.

As if to find out which of the two, Wolhie lifted her pale moonlike face and stared unabashed into her mother's face. Then, as blankly as she had looked up, she lowered her eyes slowly onto the table and picked up her spoon. And mixing a few spoonfuls of rice into the bowl of water, she scooped up a little and brought it to her mouth. Her spoon visited the saucer of soy sauce but hardly touched the *kimchi*[2]. Compared to her daughter, Eulhwa's appetite was bigger. She would mix well over half her bowlful of rice with water, and would mainly have *kimchi* as her dish. In effect, the *kimchi* was Eulhwa's dish while the soy sauce was Wolhie's.

Seeing Wolhie put down her spoon, Eulhwa pointed to her bowl and said, 'Drink the water too.'

The pale-moon face that was looking at her mother did as she was instructed and downed the water in her bowl in small gulps. Eulhwa soon followed and drank from her water bowl in one noisy slurp.

And so the breakfast came to its end. But contrary to the daily routine, Eulhwa showed no signs of getting up and clearing the table. Wolhie turned her pale-moon face towards her mother as if asking what there was left to be said. Eulhwa spoke out quite bluntly.

'I saw a bachelor ghost in my dream last night.'

Then stretching out those long slender fingers of hers, she put them on top of her head and added, 'A bachelor ghost with horns like these was trying to come into our house again and again.'

But Wolhie's face remained expressionless. She was by nature hard to unsettle or to scare.

'You understand me, don't you, my little jar.'

Eulhwa patted her daughter on the bottom. She normally called Wolhie 'Dahlie', but would sometimes call her 'princess' or 'jar'. The last seemed to refer to a honey jar or that of treasure.

'Toffee sellers and peddlers often carry bachelor ghosts. You know, don't you?'

Wolhie nodded.

Eulhwa would go out as soon as the breakfast table was cleared and would only return in the evening. Where or why she went is not known to Wolhie, nor did she want to know. Sometimes Eulhwa would come and go preparing for an exorcism, but she did not as a rule stay home, not even to wait for requests of exorcisms to perform. The reason was that she was so well known over so wide an area that she could afford not to. Indeed, for the most important 'banishment' ceremonies, the requests came in ten or fifteen days in advance while the requests for 'beckoning' ceremonies came in almost daily. Even so, there was no remuneration worth mentioning. Eulhwa regarded it instead as her duty.

Sometimes, due to her fame and reputation, requests even came in from as far as twenty kilometres away. When she did receive such requests, she did not try to wriggle out of them. Even in such cases she demanded no special treatment. Be it rice or mixed grain, she would accept whatever she was given.

'What you get won't even pay for the shoe leather,' someone would occasionally tell her. But Eulhwa would reply as if such things were of no consequence whatsoever.

'Shall I let someone die because my legs are tired?'

In fact, considering the amount of effort required to travel twenty or so kilometres on the country paths, ten times what she was getting would still have been inadequate as a just reward.

However, as generous as Eulhwa was in her services, the recipients, instead of being grateful, rather regarded them as their right. Perhaps this was because they used to pour a large bowl or two of rice into Eulhwa's collection sack when the harvest season came round. But in recent years Eulhwa had ceased to go around the village carrying her sack. Her way of thinking was unsophisticated.

'To us who could eat with food to spare on just a few grains of rice, what need is there for the collection sack? We won't starve if we were to do away with the sack.'

On days when she had no exorcisms to perform, she would visit her favourite tavern and would drink and mingle with the men.

As Eulhwa spent most of her time out, Wolhie passed the days in her room, painting and playing with the mirror. That day too, Wolhie had finished a painting of a lotus flower and was playing with the hand mirror when Eulhwa's balmy, slightly husky voice was heard from outside.

5

'My princess, my dear princess,
My jar of treasure, my sweet jar of honey . . .'
When Wolhie opened the door, Eulhwa as if overcome with
joy, lifted her slender arms and started dancing from side to side.
'The baby of the moon, the flower of the stars, my sweet jar of
honey.'
Wolhie placidly directed her gaze at the bundle wrapped in a
towel in her mother's left hand. Wolhie knew that inside was
some fruit. As much as Eulhwa liked drinking, Wolhie liked
fruit, and Eulhwa knew this better than anyone else. So, during
the seasons when fruit was plentiful, she never forgot to bring
home some apples or peaches wrapped in a towel.
When Wolhie held out her hand, Eulhwa stopped her dance
and handed over the bundle. The sun had just set over the slope
of the West hill.
'Didn't any bachelor ghosts come?'
Wolhie shook her head.
'Any toffee sellers or peddlers carrying bachelor ghosts?'
Wolhie shook her head again.
'The young woman next door, or Bun-nam?'
'N,n,nobody . . .'
Wolhie stammered in reply.
Finally relieved after learning that no one had come, Eulhwa
said as if she had expected it all along, 'That was only natural.
After I prayed so devoutly to our goddess, what ghosts would
dare set foot in our house.'
With the sun already set, Eulhwa knew that nothing further
would happen to them that day. She went into the room and got
dressed for an exorcism ceremony.

1 Ondol room = a stone-floored room heated from underneath. ('On'
means warm, 'dol' means stones.)
2 Kimchi = a vegetable sidedish essential for meals, consisting of
fermented Chinese cabbage pickled with chives, garlic,
ginger and spring onions.

Chapter Two
TWO GODS

When the young man alighted from the carriage, the road was blanketed with a thick fog-like mist, and it was difficult to tell whether the shadow cast on the ground was due to the moonlight or the dim, remote twilight after sunset.

The young man placed the black, worn-out leather bag under his left arm and adjusted the grey cap on his head with his right hand, after which he turned towards the sky and stood gazing at it for some time. The countless stars, more than ever in number, all seemed to be welcoming him after his long absence and the moon of the ninth day of the lunar month was leaning west enveloped in a thin white veil of clouds.

As he branched off into an alley from the main road, paddy fields greeted him. Then suddenly the throng of a chorus of frogs came rudely into his ear. The croaking was such that it seemed to bury the whole plain under the noise.

The young man took across the fields. The *Baekok* area of the township where his old house was located was another eight kilometres further north. Combing through those memories of when he was small, the young man managed in no time to find the trail leading to his destination but he did not hurry his steps for he was sure he would arrive home before the night was out.

As he crossed the Bukchun stream and headed into the forest, he was greeted by the brook and the marsh around it.

7

It was here, more than anywhere else, that frogs gathered in large numbers.

He stopped in his track and surrendered his ears to the racket which seemed to be the same as it had always been, and gazed emptily into the brook. It was after the moon had set so that the blackness of the brook was sprinkled with the stars up above. It almost seemed as if the frogs themselves were spitting out these tiny twinkling spots.

Because he took his time walking, gazing into the stars spewed out by frogs, by the time he reached Baekok village, dawn was drawing near. Now that he was near his home, he wasn't really concerned whether it was night or morning and sure enough, he soon found what he was looking for. But the moment he beheld his old house, he had an uneasy feeling that something was wrong.

This could have been due to the new door of the gate which wasn't there before. He could also sense that the rafters and the wooden floors had been looked after, and all these were quite unlike his mother who didn't known how to lift a finger to do anything around the house, not in ten years.

But still, this was definitely his old house and so he gave the gate a shake. The gate was bolted from the inside. He shook it a couple of times without getting a reply. Feeling he had no choice, he yelled out at the top of his voice.

'Mother.'

The young man called out in his native dialect but still there was no answer. Two, three times he called but still no answer.

This time he rattled the gate harder. Three, four times he shook the gate. At length a sound came out.

'Who is it?'

It was a man's voice.

'It's Sul, Yongsul.'

The young man replied raising his voice. Mumbles were heard from inside the house and the door burst open, and the man whose voice he'd heard asked him again.

'Who?'

'Yongsul.'

'Who's Yongsul?'

'The Yongsul who used to live in this house.'

'Oh, you mean that shaman's family?'

The word 'shaman' offended his ears but the villagers had

always called his family that and he couldn't really complain, nor was it the appropriate time or place to do so.

'Yes,' replied the young man.

'Then you must be the shaman's son.' The man half mumbled to himself.

Being called the shaman's son also hurt him but he decided to tolerate what he heard and answered as before.

'Yes, I am.'

'I'm sorry to have to tell you this at this time of night, but she moved away a long time ago.'

'Whereabouts did she go to?'

'I heard it was somewhere outside the old walls.'

'Do you know the name of the village?'

'Now, what was that called . . . Seongbat, I think.'

The man did not seem certain of the name.

Knowing it would be of no further use asking the man, the young man cordially bade farewell in standard Seoul accent.

'I'm sorry to have troubled you so late at night.'

'I'm alright but how about you? You wouldn't have a place to go to so late in the night . . .' remarked the man as if to complete the formalities.

The young man stood outside the gate looking fixedly at the stars and decided to go to the village hall. He remembered that the hall was always empty at night.

A little way in towards the village from his old house lay the mill and turning left, passing the low wall covered with creeping pumpkin stems, one came to the toilet of the village hall, always infested with buzzing flies, and next to this was the caretaker's house, and last of all, the rather solitary building built on top of a ridge was the village hall.

In one way, the fact that nothing had changed in ten years – the village, the alley way and the mill, the low wall, the fly-infested toilet, the caretaker's house and the hall itself – somehow reassured him, but at the same time, they all made him feel terribly desolate.

Entering the yard, he climbed the embankment and taking his shoes off at the foot-stone, entered the spacious wooden floored room of the village hall.

The young man took off his jacket and socks and came down to the well and washed his face, but there was not a sound from the caretaker's house.

9

. . .Everything's the same . . . thought the young man and slapped a mosquito that had landed on his cheek.

It was not until sunset the next day that the young man found his mother's house. The reason why it took so long to find the famous shaman's house had partly to do with the fact that he tried to avoid using the word 'shaman' or the name 'Eulhwa', and partly because of the fact that there were so many names for the same place, such as 'Seong-oe-ri' or 'Seong-bu-ri' apart from the name 'Seongbat' which he had heard the night before.

This neighbourhood called Seong-oe-ri or Seong-bu-ri was officially a part of the town but in reality, it was no different from any other farming community outside the town. This was not only because most of the households were engaged in farming. More than this, the probable reason it was separated from the town was because the old Wall, though crumbled down, remained distinct in the people's minds. The old fortress walls, which were no more than a pile of rubble, were still clearly distinguishable in the north and west. What was more, following the outline of the wall, an open ditch ran conspicuously along. Therefore the two possible approach routes consisted of first leaving the town at the south and following the ditch into the south eastern part of the neighbourhood, or leaving the west exit to the town, crossing the ditch at the stepping stones, and entering the neighbourhood at the north eastern side. The reason why there were so many names for this one place was due partly to its peculiar location.

The route the young man was shown was the southern one, and so he happened to enter the neighbourhood through the main road.

Seong-oe-ri had several big tile-roofed houses in the south east so that when entering from the south, it looked like a fairly rich area. But from the point where the tree dedicated to the guardian spirits was situated (in the olden days a shrine was situated next to it), and into the alley leading to the centre of the neighbourhood, all that caught the eyes of the beholder were houses with thatched roofs.

To make matters worse, since all the households were farming ones, in a corner of every yard were piles of rotting grass and straw as big as small shelters, and next to those, big gaping ditches which served as toilets, and they were all giving off a most unpleasant stench which seemed able to suffocate the whole area.

This stench got worse as one went further west. The main road running north to south divided this neighbourhood neatly into two halves, and the tile-roofed houses were mostly in the eastern half while it was difficult to find even big thatched roof houses let alone tile-roofed ones in the western half.

Even within the western half itself, the further one ventured west, the smaller the houses got and the bigger the compost heaps became, so that the stench – of urine, muck, rotting vegetation, etc. – was at its most offensive.

The shaman Eulhwa's house which the young man was looking for, was the only tile-roofed house west of the main road. But no one referred to it as the tile-roofed house. Before, they called it Granny House, and now it was known just as the shaman's house. This was not only because the 'granny' or the shaman was of more importance than the fact that it was a tile-roofed house. Although tile-roofed in name, the house was one which was ready to crumble any moment like some sinister goblin's cave. The roof tiles were so agèd that they were fleeced with green moss and in the gaps between them dust and earth had accumulated and greenish fungi reared their ugly heads. The rafters and pillars, like the roof, were also covered with dirt and soot.

The young man stood gaping at this unsightly thing before he entered the yard. Even from afar he felt his heart sink, because the house had no signs of human life whatsoever. For a start, the angular, gaunt wall surrounding the house was different from any wall he had seen. It was rather as if the old fortress walls had been moved here in a big pile of debris and since the wall was no more than a pile of rubble, there was no sign of a gate or door ever having existed there. On the eastern corner was an opening with blackish rocks one either side and this presumably served as the entrance.

However, it didn't seem as if one had to pass through this entrance. In several places the wall had crumbled completely and these gaps somehow seemed as if they had been used by someone. The young man himself at first thought of passing over the gap but changed his mind and entered through the two blackish rocks which were meant to be the door.

He stopped in his tracks once inside the walls, for the densest jungle of weeds he had ever seen confronted him and barred any progress. Unlike a patch of maize or pumpkin, it was a thick impenetrable mass of weeds. Among the tall ones were bush clovers, wild maize, and wild millet, and they towered over the wild spinach, crabgrass, ampelopses, and other nameless weeds. He had as a little boy, spent many a lonely hour in the mountain valleys and fields so that he had come to be quite familiar and indeed, friendly with wild plants but he had never come across such a dense mass of weeds before.

The young man followed the trail across the eastern side of the yard under the wall and approached the house from the front. As he got nearer he could see paintings stuck on the wall, either side of the door. From afar, the house only seemed to be a dirty, dark mass, but subsequently these coloured images covering the whole wall had started to reveal itself.

The picture on the left depicted a male figure in the most resplendent official, uniform-like costume, with a magnificent beard, and on one side it was written in Chinese characters, 'Taeju: Great Spirit of the Heavens' while on the right was a female figure dressed in the green uniform-like costume and along side this image also it was written in Chinese, 'Myongdu: the Great Goddess.' For him, he had no way of knowing what Taeju or Myongdu meant and simply presumed that they were paintings which shamans used.

He thus stood beneath the roof of the house studying the pictures and was hoping that somebody would open the door and look out, but there was no sign of people from inside the room.

He stood right up against the edge of the house and called out in the standard Seoul intonation.

'Hello.'

There was nothing.

'Hello!'

Nothing.

'Listen, is there anyone home?'

This time he called in his native dialect but still there was nothing.

12

'Look here.'

This time he tapped the wooden floor slightly but the result was the same. The wooden floor through months of neglect had gathered earth and dust till it was black.

Deciding not to sit on the wooden floor, he cried out again, this time almost shouting, and gave the door a tap at the same time.

'Isn't anyone home?'

It was only then that the door started opening and a small white face peeping out of the gap caught his eye. Immediately he guessed it was Wolhie.

. . .But how could Wolhie have such a small, white, mirror-like face . . .

As these thoughts flickered over his mind he tried hard to put on a smile but this was already after the door had been shut tight in his face.

'Hello, could you please open the door?'

The young man pleaded in his native dialect and in a soft appealing tone, but there was no response. He thought for a moment that perhaps he should call her name and tell her who he was, but then he changed his mind, for ten years had elapsed since he saw her last and it was doubtful if she even remembered him.

Yongsul had to simply wait till his mother came. But till then, there was no place where he could rest sitting down. The wooden floor was black with earth and dust and the yard was a thick mass of weeds, and on top of this the ground was damp due perhaps to a blocked sewage drain, and from the moss-eaten earth, an acrid smell offended his nose.

Having come this far, he decided to have a look round and turned the corner of the house but the house was completely surrounded by weeds on all four sides and he dared not venture into the thick jungle for he didn't know how many poisonous snakes and insects lurked there. But standing right up against the edge of the weeds he leaned forward and looked at the side of the house. The east-facing wall had also been painted on. The pictures on the front wall had been those painted on thick paper which had then been stuck on the wall. But the paintings on this east-facing wall were frescoes, directly painted on the wall. The images it depicted were similar to the 'Four Spirits' images one found in Buddhist temples, but the

Chinese characters above the images read, 'Sky god', 'Mountain god' and so on. But the pictures themselves (as well as the characters) were so old and bleached by sunlight, and so dark from the dirt that only the faintest outlines were visible. Also, the fact that the wall had crumbled away in certain parts did not help matters.

But still, the pictures showed a maturity of handling, and they had a strange power to tell the observer of fabulous events of ages past.

Yongsul's experiences in Buddhist temples told him that these paintings were usually painted over three faces of the house – the sides and back – and thus a similar painted wall would exist at the back as well. But not being able to plough his way through the weeds, he turned round.

It was at that very moment when a woman's voice came from the front of the yard.

'Oh, who could that be? Who could it be?'

Yongsul looked round. It was Eulhwa.

Eulhwa lifted her arm as if executing a dancing motion and pointed to him, scolding him in a chant.

'Who could that be? Who is it that is in someone else's house like a thief or some ghost?'

Yongsul simply wore a radiant smile on the white, neatly carved face of his and faced Eulhwa. He couldn't think of anything to say. She pierced him with her glistening eyes.

'This is the house of the daughter of the Great Goddess where no thieves nor ghosts can dare enter. If you are a passing traveller, go away peacefully. If you are a blind thief, crawl away quickly, and if you are a ghost who's lost his way, out you go down through the sewer.'

Eulhwa commanded in a tone half threatening, half persuading.

'Mother, I'm neither ghost nor thief.'

'Then you must be a passing traveller.'

'No mother, I'm not a traveller either.'

Yongsul's face lit up with a smile and his voice was calm and soft.

'Who is this "mother"? If you aren't a traveller, what could you be?'

'Mother, I'm Yongsul, your son.'

'What? . . . Am I your mother?'

14

Eulhwa at first had not realized what the stranger had meant by 'mother' because he had spoken in a strange dialect, but it soon reached her that this strange young man was calling her his mother.

'Yes, you are my mother. I'm your son, Yongsul.'

She was still not sure what was happening.

'Yes mother, I'm the Yongsul whom you sent to Kirim Temple ten years ago.'

'Kirim Temple?'

Her eyes twinkled once more. It seemed as though the name of this temple was more meaningful than the name Yongsul itself.

To her, Kirim temple was the most sacred place on earth, an abode of wizards, and she had always hoped she would one day return there. At the same time, the memory of ten years ago came flooding back, when she took the ten year old Yongsul by the hand to leave him with a monk she knew there.

'You mean Kirim Temple?'

'Yes, mother. It was Kirim Temple. The first place you took me to.'

'Then you mean you're Yongsul?'

Her voice had now changed completely. No longer was she chanting in a threatening tone but was speaking softly as any woman would. At the same time, colour seemed to flow back into her face.

'Mother!'

Yongsul let the little black bag drop from under his arm and rushed into the woman's arms.

'Ah my son. Sul, are you Sul?'

She opened wide her arms and embraced her son.

'Yongsul, what are you doing here?'

Tears came rolling down her cheeks as she held her son in her breast. This was the first time ever that she had shed tears in her own mind, that is, not possessed with some spirit.

It was while her face was still wet with tears that Wolhie opened the door and came out barefoot. And upon seeing the two figures clasped in each other's arms, she was so frightened that she grew pale on the spot shaking. The stranger in her mother's arms was definitely that goblin which had tapped the wooden floor and shaken the door a little while ago. What could have happened . . . Was her mother completely possessed by the goblin? Why else would she be embracing it like that . . .

Wolhie approached a couple of steps trying hard to control her shaky legs.

. . .Ah, mummy's face, it's wet. What's happened? . . .

'Mum, Mummy . . . Goblin?' said Wolhie, pointing at Yongsul.

Eulhwa slowly shook her head, her face still wet from the tears, telling her daughter he wasn't. Eulhwa pointed to the young man and spoke to her, whose fear and surprise had not subsided.

'It's your brother.'

'Brother?'

Wolhie's face was now full of a new surprise and wonder. It was extremely rare for Wolhie to ever inquire like this into events around her with her broken speech, but this only went to show how important an event this must have been to her.

'Yes, the brother who left us to go into the temple when you were six. He is brother Sul.'

'Brother S-u-l?'

In answer to this question Eulhwa simply nodded her head a little. Yongsul put on a refreshing smile.

'Yes, your brother. As I said, the one who left home when you were six.'

Wolhie still seemed uncertain of what was happening and merely stared into Yongsul's face.

'Let's go inside. Go in the room and have a rest.'

At these words, Yongsul picked up the small leather bag from the ground. By accident both Eulhwa and Wolhie directed their gaze on this worn out bag which revealed white patches where the leather had been worn through. This was not because of any expectation that it could have been some kind of magic bag, full of jewels or gems. Rather, it was because this little thing was the sole possession on this mysterious stranger who called himself 'son' and 'brother'.

Placing the bag under his left arm, he followed his mother inside. Wolhie, who was a step ahead ran barefoot from the yard onto the wooden floor and then into the room without seeming to care in the least about getting her feet dirty.

. . .How can such a beautiful and well mannered girl go

16

round barefoot from the yard into the house . . .

With these thoughts he straightened Wolhie's straw shoes on the shoe-stone, and started untying his own shoe laces. His boots were long leather ones which needed untying every time he took them off.

When Yongsul went up the wooden floor and opened the door, he was again thrown into confusion and consternation by two things. One was the utter chaos inside the room and the other was Wolhie.

Wolhie who had gone in only a moment before was changing her clothes with the door of the chest wide open. She seemed to be taking off the green *chima* and *jogori* and putting on blue ones. When Yongsul opened the door, the blue *chima* and *jogori* were on the table and she was taking off her bloomers. He shut the door and turned round immediately, but for one moment he had unknowingly gazed at the beautifully sculptured body of Wolhie, as if carved out of jade, and the image did not disappear out of his head. He had seen paintings when at the church but he reckoned that he had never seen a body more beautiful than the one he saw just now.

But he wished these thoughts would leave him swiftly, since the fact that one thought of the nude body of a woman was proof of one's capitulation to the Devil's temptation. What's more, to think that the body was none other than that of his half sister, Yongsul couldn't suppress the feeling of guilt inside him.

So, as if to fix his attention somewhere else, he focused his eyes on the dark paintings stuck on the front wall – the ones of 'Taeju' and 'Myongdu'. As he stood wondering who could have painted them and how, and for what purpose, the door opened a little and Wolhie in her blue dress peeped out and called him.

'Brother.'

Yongsul, guilty at having seen his sister's body, though it was unintentional, couldn't look Wolhie straight in the face as he entered the room.

The room itself was on the wide side but the altar stood on the north-facing wall, and on either side stood two wooden chests. The big one on the left, judging from the fact that this was the one from where Wolhie took out her blue dress, seemed to be the one where her clothes were kept, and the small one on the right seemed to contain Eulhwa's ceremonial costumes, hat, fans, and other objects of the sort.

Except for this north-facing wall, the other three walls were covered with brightly coloured paintings. Among these, the biggest one carried eight Chinese characters meaning 'Great Goddess', and judging from this, Yongsul guessed that it must be his mother's tutelary spirit. Apart from this, there were pictures similar to those on the outside called 'Spirit King' and 'Great Spirit' along with bluebirds and lotus blossoms which had been incorporated into the design.

Yongsul had to acknowledge that these wild and gaudy paintings were all to do with his mother's profession, but seeing the total confusion and Wolhie's apparent indifference to the black swarm of flies on the paintings, he himself felt somewhat embarrassed and ashamed. But Yongsul promised himself that he would change all this little by little, and closing his eyes he prayed in silence.

. . . Dear God, our Father, I am ever grateful for your guidance sending this unworthy son to his mother. You have given your son the best possible place for him to carry on your work. I pray thee, let me not give up half way or be disheartened, and give your blessing with your watchful eye now and ever more . . .

Seeing Yongsul pray to himself with his eyes closed, Wolhie, as if thinking he was tired and sleepy from the long journey, passed him the dirty pillow from the chest.

Yongsul pushed the pillow back in front of Wolhie.

'No, Wolhie, I'm not sleepy.'

Eulhwa came in carrying the supper table. On the table were three bowls of rice, three bowls of cold water, a small bowl of *kimchi* and a plate of soy sauce. It was exactly the same as the breakfast table except for the fact that there was one more bowl of rice with one more bowl of water and another set of spoons and chopsticks. 'Come on, you must be hungry. Help yourself,' Eulhwa said handing her son the spoon.

But Yongsul did not start eating and seemed to hesitate. Seeing this Eulhwa, mistakenly thinking that it was because of the plainness of the meal said,

'I told you a little while ago, remember? This is a temple as well. Didn't you have plain meals at your temple?'

18

'No, it's not because of that, mother.'

Yongsul lifted his head and glanced at his mother.

'*Kimchi* is just fine,'

'Then help yourself, and don't just sit there staring at your food.'

Saying this, Eulhwa took up her spoon. But before she scooped the first spoonful, she glanced once more at Yongsul and saw his head bowed down a little and his lips moving. It was certain to her that he was reciting an incantation. That moment a dark shadow flickered over her face and a touch of indignation shrouded her.

'Do you chant spells in Buddha worship before eating?'

In her eyes could be seen the fire of indignation. She always referred to Buddhism as Buddha worship and obviously she still thought he had come directly from the temple. Yongsul had not shaven his head nor was he wearing the Buddhist gown. Indeed, he was wearing a western style jacket with leather shoes, and even a cap. But Eulhwa was of a peculiar temperament which disregarded outer looks completely.

Opening his eyes, Yongsul slowly lifted his head and caught her face.

'Mother, I'm not a Buddha worshipper.'

'Not a Buddha worshipper?'

'Mother, I am Christian.'

'What? Christian worship?'

Eulhwa's voice had become rougher and higher in pitch.

'Yes mother. In Kirim Temple and other temples I became disillusioned with Buddhism and became a Christian.'

'What do you mean you didn't like Buddha worship. What other worship is greater?'

'While I was at the temple, I saw the good honest monks doing nothing but sleep all day and night, and the not so honest ones busy doing business for themselves. That's why I began to dislike Buddhism.'

The expression on his face as he spoke was mild and his voice was gentle. There was not a hint of any confrontation with his mother. Rather, he seemed to be begging his mother for understanding.

At the softness of her son's reply, the apparent anger seemed to cool down somewhat, and she said in a calmer tone, 'Well, what could you have known. You were only ten. But

19

why do you offend the Buddha by saying whether Buddha worship is good or bad?'

There was sarcasm in her voice.

'Mother, I was ten when I entered Kirim Temple but I studied Buddhism till I was fifteen.'

'If everyone can master Buddha worship at fifteen, then everyone in the world would become masters. Alright, even if you were tired of Buddha worship, why did you have to go and pick up that damn westerners' Jesu worship?'

'Mother, it's not Jesu worship. It's Christianity.'

Eulhwa remained silent, her angry eyes riveted on her son. But regardless of this Yongsul continued in his calm clear voice, almost as if trying to comfort his mother.

'Mother, Christianity is the worldwide religion which gives everyone of us light and life.'

To Eulhwa, 'light and life' and 'worldwide religion' were terms she could not, and indeed, need not understand.

'And who is it that's going to give us all these things?'

She referred to 'light and life' as 'these things', for she could neither understand the terms nor wanted to remember them.

Quickly catching what his mother was getting at, Yongsul said confidently,

'God gives them to us.'

'God?' asked Eulhwa in anger. 'God' was a term used by shamans like her, and it offended and disgusted her to hear Yongsul, an outsider, refer her God to something in Christianity.

Untroubled by his mother's anger, Yongsul went on in his soft and mild voice.

'Yes mother, God in Heaven above. The God who made man and all things around us.'

His calm and peaceful voice was full of pride and confidence.

Eulhwa, as if what her son said was ludicrous and pitiable gave a snigger and replied,

'That is what we call the Harvest god or the Guardian god.'

'Mother, the Harvest god and the Guardian god are no more than idols invented by the people.'

The word 'idol' made Eulhwa lose her temper. She had heard the term 'idol' from Shilgun's mother and was aware that it carried contemptuous connotations.

'How dare you! "Idols", indeed.'

Yongsul did not reply. He was tactful enough to know that to answer back would surely add to her anger.

'It seems you are a bachelor ghost.'

Eulhwa stared at Yongsul and calmly passed judgement.

'No mother, I'm your son Yongsul.'

'A bachelor ghost has possessed my son Yongsul. There's a bachelor ghost inside you.'

Saying this, Eulhwa put down her spoon on the water bowl. Apparently she had no intentions of sharing a meal with a son possessed by a devil. Immediately, Wolhie who had been watching the conversation between mother and son, followed suit and also put her spoon against the bowl of water. Yongsul was by now regretting he had used such strong terms like idol and tried to appease his mother.

'Mother, please calm down. I came to you because I missed you, and I am here so that I can look after you. Do you remember when you took me by the hand to Kirim Temple? you said, "Sul, don't think of your mother but obey the monks and become a great master."'

At this plea, Eulhwa seemed to loosen up. It seemed as if she could vividly recall the events of ten years ago. Yongsul continued.

'That time mother, you said this to me. "When you become great, don't bother looking for your mother. Your living alone would be better than being despised as a shaman's son. But if you find life unbearably hard, come and search for your mother. Together with Dalhie (Wolhie), we three can live together. Wherever you are, I'll be praying to the great Spirit for you . . ." I have never forgotten these words of yours no matter where I went. But the reason I came searching for you wasn't because my life was hard. I happened to meet a western missionary and received a lot of help and teaching and live happier than any prince or wealthy man in the world. In fact, I was so happy that I wanted to seek you again. I couldn't suppress the wish to share my happiness with my mother and sister. And so I managed to get the missionary's permission, and here I am. Please don't chide me mother. I will listen to your every wish, and I only want to be your strength.'

Yongsul stretched out his hands as he spoke, and Eulhwa,

21

without hesitation grabbed hold of them and said in a tearful voice,

'My dear son . . . how well you remember these things. If it were not for that goblin inside you, this would be the happiest event of my life.'

Thus the confrontation between mother and son was averted.

However, even while Eulhwa was in the kitchen washing up, she could not get over the fact that, to her, Yongsul's Christianity was weird, distasteful and even insulting.

. . . How has that fine boy ever become one of these Jesu-worshippers, and is that the best he could do when he supposedly came back to help his mother? . . . tut tut . . .

Eulhwa, as was her daily routine, finished the simple washing up and came into the room. The lamp in one corner of the room was but a dish of oil with a flame. Yongsul leaned against the wall with his eyes closed.

'How tired you must be after such a long journey. Lie there. We are going to sleep soon.'

'No mother it's alright, I'm not tired.'

'Don't call me that in such a strange accent. It's bad. Why don't you call me Mum in your own dialect.'

Eulhwa protested in a somewhat concerned voice.

'It's not anything bad mother. They say that up north, and sometimes I can't help using the term. But if you find it unpleasant I will stop calling you that.'

'It *is* bad. Why do you have to throw away the words that are yours and pick up strange words from somewhere else? The people who do are often rude and unkind.'

'I understand mother. I think I'll sleep in that room.'

Yongsul was pointing to the room with the large altar. Eulhwa did not speak but simply shook her head. She explained.

'Not everyone can go into that room.'

Her answer was curt and there was no further argument. Eulhwa got up and took down a mattress and a pillow from the top of the chest. Yongsul recognised them as being definitely those used by Wolhie's father.

. . . I wonder where he's gone. Surely I wouldn't be given a dead person's mattress . . .

22

Yongsul prayed in silence once more still leaning against the wall and finally lay down to sleep.

The next day after breakfast, Eulhwa told Yongsul as if warning him,

'Don't touch anything in this house, be it inside or in the yard or anywhere. If you do, bad things will happen. I'm going to Master Chung's house.'

After Eulhwa left the house Yongsul asked Wolhie of her father's whereabouts.

'Where is your father?'

Wolhie seemed to panic at this question and stared back at him.

'You know, your father when we used to live in the Jatshil neighbourhood.'

'Over there . . .'

Wolhie was pointing East.

'Where is that?'

'G-a-p-o.'

'You mean Gampo?'

Wolhie nodded.

'When?'

Wolhie seemed to think for a while and counted nine on her fingers. Presumably it meant that her father left when she was nine.

'Don't you miss him?'

'He came.'

'When? Does he come often?'

Wolhie shook her head.

'I'll go and bring him back soon.'

Wolhie didn't answer. It was not certain whether she didn't understand him or whether she felt afraid of what her mother would say.

In the evening, Eulhwa came back with some plums for Wolhie and two dried pollacks and some bean sprouts for supper. It was rare for her to bring home food like this. It only happened perhaps a couple of times a year. But Yongsul who had gone out that day was not back yet.

'Where did your brother say he was going?'

Wolhie only shook her head.

'When did he go out?'

'Afternoon.'

23

Eulhwa was surprised at how clear her pronunciation of the word 'afternoon' had been.

'Did he take that little bag?'

To Eulhwa, that 'little bag' had been gnawing at her mind ever since Yongsul's arrival. Wolhie simply stared back. The small bag was nowhere to be found in the room.

. . . So he did take it. What kind of magic could be in there, I wonder. Would he try to keep it secret from his mother? I think he's trying to hide something. It is all probably because of that demon Jesu. Our Sul, he used to be so good and kind. If only he had stayed at the temple, he would surely have become a master by now. Oh, and how he cried when I told him we had to part . . . If he had been blessed with better parents he would surely have become a great man.

Eulhwa drowned herself in her thoughts and recollections.

Chapter Three
THE RIVER GOD

Eulhwa had given birth to Yongsul when she was no more than a fifteen year old girl. That is, she was not married and the father of the child was none other than the young man with the scruffy hair who lived next door. But this is not to say they were lovers or in any amorous relationship. All that lay separating the two houses was a solitary fence and as a result, the two households came to know each other as well as they knew themselves. However, it did not look as if the bundle of unkempt hair particularly fancied her nor of course did he get up to any tricks.

It so happened that in that particular year the hot pepper paste of the young man's house was celebrated for its taste, and Eulhwa's house too had begged a couple of platefuls. Eulhwa herself enjoyed it immensely.

Her real name, before she acquired the name Eulhwa, was Oksun.

'Mum, when you go working for Chool's house again, could you ask for another plateful of pepper paste?' Oksun asked her mother licking the last traces of pepper paste still on the plate.

'Chool' was short for Sungchool, the young man with the untidy hair next door. Her mother cast a reproachful glance from her tired face, red with over-exposure.

'Are you really going to behave like that? It's not right that a girl should think about nothing else but eating.'

Oksun herself could see that to go round to someone else's house for the third time to beg pepper paste would be betraying all sense of shame.

The next day about lunch time she was returning home after gathering some wild vegetables from the mountain. She bumped into Chool straddling across a dyke having his lunch. The route from the hills to the village was such that one could not avoid passing this dyke. Seeing Oksun approach him, Sungchool greeted her with a big smile.

'Well, look who's here! Come and join me for lunch.'

'You must be hungry. Don't let me disturb you.'

Oksun refused the offer but for a second she threw down a glance at the lunch Chool had spread out on the ground.

There lay a bowlful of boiled rice and a tempting saucerful of the famous pepper paste. Oksun felt her mouth water but she turned her head and tried to walk past. At that moment Chool sprang to his feet and grabbed the vegetable basket and finally succeeded in seating Oksun on the ground.

'There's nothing to feel ashamed of. After all we're neighbours. Please have lunch with me.'

Oksun only gave back an awkward smile. Her face was tinted with embarrassment.

'What if someone sees us?'

'There's no one to see us in these hills, and even if anyone did, so what? What's wrong with next door neighbours sharing lunch together?'

Chool swiftly rinsed his spoon and chopsticks and handed them to Oksun.

'You needn't go to all that trouble for me. Have your lunch,' answered Oksun, awkwardly accepting the spoon and chopsticks.

Chool, as if to reassure her, stood up and fashioned a pair of chopsticks with his sickle from a branch of the bush clover next to him.

'There, here are my chopsticks.'

The situation having arrived at this, she judged that it would be even more embarrassing for her to refuse further, and she began to eat as she had been offered. After she took some rice and also some hot pepper, Chool put down the twigs and said in self-satisfaction.

'I had a lot before you came.'

26

When Oksun tried to follow suit and put down her chopsticks too, Chool reacted with some anger.

'Are you really going to be like that?'

Oksun had no choice but to clean up every morsel of food.

Sungchool, as if relieved, chipped in another comment as if to complete the formalities.

'Thanks for sharing such plain food with me.'

'I guess you'd had no trouble with preparing dishes at your house with your tasty pepper paste . . .' Oksun said, trying to return the compliment.

'If it's our pepper paste you want, I'll get it for you as much as you like.'

'You'll only get told off by your mother.'

'I'll pass it to you through the hole in the fence when my mother isn't home.'

On seeing Sungchool speak, there was for a second a sudden flash in Oksun's eyes, and Sungchool was arrested by its strange inexplicable power. Without knowing he grabbed Oksun's wrist. And it was not certain who it was that gave his or her lips first; lips still red with the pepper paste, and the two still holding each other's sleeves, started rolling down, down towards the field of green barley, maturing in the early summer air.

When Oksun's stomach started swelling, she and her mother left the village. This was not as much out of any sense of shame but because their immediate livelihood was being threatened.

Originally, Oksun had been born at a village built on a junction popularly known as Yokchon (the station village), which was about six or so kilometres away.

Oksun's father was the son of a station hand. Although he was engaged in farming by name, he was a rascal who enjoyed gambling far more than any work in the field, and had been stabbed to death in a brawl when Oksun was no more than two years old.

Having her husband killed in such a terrible way was too much for Oksun's mother. She sold her tiny thatched house and the narrow strip of paddy field cut out of the mountain, and moved to this house in Bamnamutgol (the chestnut tree village).

This small community was no different from hundreds of

others but it was the pride of the inhabitants that it was a village of virtuous, hard-working farmers and it was not hard to foresee that someone from a notorious place as Yokchon and with such a macabre tale to tell would not be a welcome guest. But the newcomer was a frail woman with a child to look after. Also, when they saw that she was a sober and unpretentious woman, they did not go out of their way to goad or harrass her.

As time passed, the mother and daughter came to receive the sympathy of all the inhabitants. But they were still left with nothing to eat. Soon it became something of a village custom to help this poor woman, and the only way this could be done was to call her when there was anything that needed done around the house. It thus happened that Oksun's mother was dragged here and there and eventually ended up as the resident village work hand.

In the ten years spent going from house to house she acquired and further consolidated her reputation as a quiet, stealthy, hard worker, but she was never treated on equal terms with the rest of the villagers.

On top of this situation Oksun's pregnancy further worsened their reputation. The villagers had reached the verdict that she was different from them by nature.

Separated from the villagers, Oksun and her mother had no means of survival. With no possessions they could call their own, their very existence was put in jeopardy. On top of this, Sungchool's family lit another fire by pleading them to move somewhere else for the sake of their family name. At first they promised to pay for the moving expenses but later ended up by promising to pay for a whole new house to move into.

The place provided by Sungchool's family was another little house by the road at a Y-junction in Yokchon, the village from where they had fled ten years ago. Oksun herself could see that she could no longer live in the chestnut village, and with not a soul to welcome them anywhere, what other alternative was there but to accept it.

To Oksun's mother it was a place of bitterness and rancor, but in the ten years she had been away everything had changed. Also she was not in a position to look back at her past. This was so much so that it was as hard to get odd jobs here as it would have been in any village to which she was a stranger.

It was then that someone came and suggested they open a tavern. The situation was pretty hopeless with Oksun's stomach growing bigger by the day and with no way to support themselves. They took up the advice and began selling drinks by the roadside. The house being situated near the Y-junction of the village, there were enough clients for the two women to make a living.

Oksun gave birth when they had at last reached the stage when they could thus stop worrying about their daily bread. It was a boy. All who saw the baby said in admiration how handsome it was, as if carved out of jade. To Oksun's mother, the cause of all that grief and anxiety had suddenly and quite unexpectedly become a source of great happiness and joy. Whenever she looked at the baby, her heart began beating faster and she was filled with love, joy and happiness. She was not sure why or from where these emotions sprang forth.

Compared with her mother, Oksun herself was quite calm. She did not seem to think of her son as a blessing descended from the heavens, as her mother obviously did. Indeed, she seemed almost too mature to be a sixteen-year-old mother. She had grown out of her indiscreet and wild temperament, and played an admirable role as mother.

'What shall we call the baby?'

One day, quite unexpectedly Oksun's mother posed this question.

'Yongsul,' replied Oksun without a moment's hesitation. Apparently she had thought of the child's name beforehand.

'Clever little thing. She must be really fond of her child though she tries to look uninterested on the outside. Why else would she have given a name for it already . . .'

But her mother did not realize why the particular name 'Yongsul' was given. Had she recognized how similar the name 'Yongsul' was to the name 'Sungchool', she would have realized how much her daughter was still thinking about the father of the child – the young man with the scruffy hair.

In the years Oksun's mother spent in the chestnut tree village, she had never once sent her daughter out to work though she herself toiled away as a village workhand. In the same way, she never allowed her daughter to serve drinks at the drinking tables. Indeed, though Oksun was no more than a wench with a fatherless child, it was her mother's firm belief that mother and daughter could not serve at the drinking tables, pouring wine together and degrading themselves. And in accordance with her wishes, Oksun never once came on to the drinking tables to serve. Instead, she took charge of the other chores which needed to be done in and around the tavern – the steaming of rice, preparing *kimchi*, doing the washing, and others.

This care soon brought its results. The story of Oksun and her son soon spread even to the neighbouring villages, and she, though an unmarried mother with a fatherless child, was regarded more with sympathy than with disapproval. After all, was it not all in the stars that she meet such a fate? It said at first how good-natured Oksun was, as was her mother, but soon people began to rate her over and above her mother, and at length it reached the stage where people began saying how flawless Oksun was in all aspects of her character.

With all this praise it was only a matter of time before the talk of marriage began floating around. The first offer was for a concubine to a childless house and then a matchmaker's offer came in of a second wife. Oksun's mother did not give the first offer any serious consideration but the second subsequent offer seemed to interest her.

'Why don't you ask her yourself? No sensible thing would get married just because her mother told her so,' said Oksun's mother to the matchmaker, showing subdued interest.

Although Oksun's mother had remained uncommitted, there was no reason in the world why she could not talk to her daughter. When she did suggest the match, intimating that she was in favour, the answer from Oksun was not of flat refusal.

'What about Yongsul?'

She seemed to be implying that were it not for Yongsul it would be fine with her.

'What are you worrying about? I'll look after Yongsul. Do you think I could survive without seeing our Yongsul?'

To this confident answer from her mother, there were no more words from Oksun. She had more or less consented to the mother's wish. The house to which Oksun was to enter as the second wife was that of a middle-aged man, fifty one years old, who lived in the fashionable part of the village. The family was a relatively wealthy one and had two grown up sons and a daughter. It would, of course, have been better if Oksun were to have entered the house of a more vigorous, healthy husband but to wait for an opportunity like that was too daunting a prospect. So Oksun's mother decided not to let go of the opportunity and flashed the sign of assent to the matchmaker.

It was in this way that the nineteen year old girl became second wife to a late middle-aged man. Although her background was not noble and her family was not of any distinguished birth, Oksun was pleasant in her own way. Her fine looks, good temperament, and her skilful hands soon bought the love of her husband and also managed not to incur the displeasure of the first wife's sons and daughters.

But as if the love of her husband was too intense, the fifty one year old man began to cough violently as he reached his fifty second year. Oksun could sense that the illness was not something to be taken lightly and she did everything in her power to make him better – boiling down all those things said to be good for the body – the corncrake, eels, terrapins, and refusing the bed though it pained her to do so. For two years he had been bed-ridden and finally in the fifty fourth year of his life he passed away betraying the constant and tearful nursing of Oksun.

For Oksun it was impossible for her not to make love to the old husband but afterwards she had done everything in her power to save her husband's life; in the preparation of food, the constant nursing, and more. Indeed, she had been flawless in her duties as a wife. But inevitably the fingers pointed to her as the cause of death, by the daughters of the first wife and even by the neighbours and occupants of the house. The only understanding came from the eldest son of the house. He had heard the dying words of his father telling to take good care of his poor second wife widowed before her time. The son would scold his sisters saying,

'Don't go uttering things which would drive nails into someone's heart!'

After the old man's death Oksun stayed shut up in her room. She could not face the family for guilt, and she had not as yet thought of what she would do or how she was to live on.

Then something happened to add insult to injury. In the winter after her husband's death, a misfortune struck to rub salt into the already sore wound. Her mother who had lived without too much hardship in the house by the junction died of food poisoning after having globefish soup.

Oksun dashed over to the tavern and fainted on the spot clinging to the dead body of her mother. Onlookers managed to get her round by pouring hot water into her mouth but from that time on, she did nothing else but flood tears and sit around as if she had lost her mind.

After seeing through the funeral of her mother, Oksun locked herself in her room and was never seen to come out. The wife of the eldest son came to visit once in a while and people assumed that her late husband's house was providing her with at least something to survive.

Also during this time, people came to her suggesting she open up the tavern again. They came with arguments saying that there would be more clients than ever before were she to open up, and that her late husband's house would not support her indefinitely and she would have to look for a way to support herself. But to all these suggestions, Oksun simply shook her head, and said,

'Are you suggesting that I would starve?'

She also refused by saying:

'I don't want our Yongsul to be known as the wine seller's son.'

In the Spring of the year after, Oksun moved house without consulting anyone. It was later revealed that someone had come and offered to buy the house and Oksun had asked no more for the house than a roof over their heads, money being of no consequence. It was in this way that Oksun acquired the house at Jatshil four kilometres away.

Upon hearing this news the eldest son came running to find that the new house was barely worth half the one by the junction. He went to the person concerned and protested that it was unfair and managed to get a vegetable patch to go with the house. Oksun was glad saying that she and her son could eat off the vegetable patch but the son was rueful, moaning that it would be insulting to him and his family honour especially in the eyes of the villagers for her to live in such conditions.

After the son left Oksun praised the son for his concern and was reminded that a family with honour was somehow different from the rest. That evening Oksun took her son to the vegetable patch and made preparations to plant some seeds.

It was later that very night. Yongsul developed a fever and fell severely ill. At first she thought it was a bad cold or an attack of indigestion but the next day people living nearby came and said it looked suspiciously like smallpox. She consulted other people and got the same answer. Her eyes welled up with tears. One neighbour told her that this illness would become worse if she were to court unlucky events and told her to stay clear of any funerals or ceremonial rites.

Oksun was in agony. She had heard that smallpox was a disease which would leave half its victims dead or with pock-marked faces, and she knew that she could not live without her son.

For three days and nights Oksun never once left her son's side. One morning, the thought suddenly struck her that she must go and pray to the spirits. She left that very moment and went to the shrine she knew, about two kilometres away at Eulhwa-gol (Eulhwa village).

At the shrine she rubbed her palms and bowed praying that her son might recover from the illness. When she had completed about her thirteenth bow, she imagined she heard a voice telling her to go to Pakji. Pakji was the name of the local shaman who was given her name because of her pock-marked face.

. . . Ah, this must be the spirits telling me how I can save my Sul . . .

These were her thoughts as she hurried to visit the shaman.

After listening to Oksun, Pakji had no hesitation in saying, 'This is the work of the great spirit holding on to the life line of your son', and added that the great spirit would save her son's life and had sent Oksun to her for this to be achieved.

Oksun let out a sigh of relief.

'I'm going to leave all my trust here.'

Oksun referred to Pakji as 'here' since Oksun herself was only twenty years old and she could not call this woman, older than her mother, 'you' as the others did.

'Of course you must trust me. Who else can you trust? Go back home and prepare for a ceremony with a rush mat and some food.'

As the shaman had told her Oksun started preparing the

offerings for the exorcism rite as soon as she reached home. She managed to get a rush mat, that not without effort as she had to beg how a life was at stake. But even with the mat, there remained the problem of getting food for the ceremony. Though it was no more than a small rite she would at least have to provide a dried pollack and a plate or two of fruit but she was in no position to go to the market over four kilometres away leaving the sick child all alone unattended. What was more, the illness being no less than smallpox, the neighbours tried to avoid coming into contact with her and her son, and it was thus doubly difficult for her to ask her neighbours for a favour. But in a matter of life or death, things such as face-saving and dignity were as good as non-existent. So she went to the place she thought most generous and pleaded how a good deed would never be forgotten. That house advised her to go to Mr Oh's house, a dealer in dried food of all kinds who held a stall at the market. Thanking her neighbour for the information Oksun went straight to Oh's house and managed to buy a dried pollack, a leg of octopus, and some dried persimmon, dates and chestnuts, and came running home fearing something might have happened in her absence.

Opening the door, she saw Yongsul looking at her with eyes which looked sore as if they had been scorched in hot water.

'Sul can you see who it is? Can you see my face?'

Sul did not answer but simply blinked his eyes once.

'Sul, just hang on there for a little longer. I'll make you well in no time.'

Coming outside, Oksun started pounding the rice she had left to soak a little while earlier. She used the mortar because she felt that she couldn't go to the neighbour's mill just to pound a handful of grain. From the rice powder she baked some heavy rice bread and afterwards washed out the rice pot and began preparing the rice to be used in the ceremony. Having done all she believed was in her power to do she let out a long sigh. The shaman Pakji arrived in the evening.

Oksun spread the mat and brought in the table she had prepared earlier. The shaman took one look at the table and tutted her tongue as if she pitied the plainness of the offering. She took a long close look at Yongsul and surveyed the room anew.

'They do say that sincerity can move Heaven. After all, the

34

spirits won't be any fuller in the stomach if you had prepared more.'

Seating herself on the floor, Pakji undid the sack she was carrying and produced some bells, a gong, and a fan.

Opening the fan, Pakji waved it several times over the offering and then moved it over Yongsul's face. Yongsul opened his eyes and looked attentively at the fan. Capturing Yongsul's attention, she moved on to the mat and slowly opened her mouth, her arms still stretched towards the table.

'Guest*, where are you from?
You must be from the Great Land in the South
The land where the hundred crops grow rich
Where millet of all kinds and maize and corn
Flourish and thrive
The melons, water melons, pumpkins, gourds
Bear fruit in bunches
Where cherries, plums, grapes, persimmons, wild grapes,
wild berries, pears, apples, peaches, balsam-pears, citrons,
pomegranates, soapberries, chestnuts, dates,
Are plentiful, but still rice is rare.
Our land, Korea is the Land of the Morning Calm,
The land where the sun rises, the land of the Diamond
mountain and the silken mountains.
The rice here is jade white
Washing and cooking it we have snow-white hard boiled rice
One bowl for the grown-up, one for the child,
One bowl for the woman, one for the man,
One bowl for the old and one for the young
The water is clear and people are hospitable
When the guest from the South was coming to our
Korea. . .'

At this moment the shaman put down the fan and picked up the gong. As she struck the brass with a piece of deer horn it made a clear metallic sound.

'Your clothes are clothes of paper
Your hat is of paper and so are your shoes
Your socks are of paper and so is your cloak

When you were crossing the Han river, the Nam river, the
Nakdong, the Chungshon
You called to the boatman telling him to make ready the
boat
But the boatman did not listen to you
Saying that his boat was made of earth and rock
And would not float on the water.
You were so angry that your hair stood on end
And walked onto the water in your paper cloak and your
paper shoes
And crossed the river in your paper cloak and your paper
shoes
Without getting a single drop of water on yourself
So you came to see the Land of the Silken Mountains, the
Diamond mountain, Baegdu mountain, To-am mountain,
Sundo mountain, and other famous sites.
Meeting notable characters from each household
Precious sons, Princes and counts, Princesses and countesses,
And when you went around meeting man and woman, old
and young
Giving them marks on their faces
As if puffed with powder, stipled with rouge,
In houses of sincerity
You give red dots holding a red book
And in houses without sincerity
You give black dots holding a black book.
But this house is imploring you to clear its waters
And is trying to please you with its sincerity.
The first and second day to the East,
Third, fourth to the South,
Fifth, sixth to the West,
Seventh, eighth to the North,
And ninth, tenth back to where you came.
Please take notice of the sincerity of this house
And clear the waters for this precious boy, Yongsul born in
the year of the horse
Dear great guest from the South
When you are returning to that place where the mountains
are beautiful and the water is clear,
Nourish yourself with the food this house has provided, and
Clear the waters and return to where you came from.'

36

The shaman gave another tap on the gong and picked up the fan once more. Capturing Yongsul's attention she moved the fan over the table for the last time and finally waved it out of the room.

After the exorcism was over, Pakji advised Oksun while packing her things back into the kerchief bundle.

'He'll be fine tomorrow. You needn't worry about the fee. I'll come and collect it whenever you can afford it. In the meantime don't hesitate to call me if there is anything bothering you.'

Although the shaman had not received any remuneration or reward from Oksun, she nevertheless treated her with great generosity.

As Pakji had predicted, Yongsul's breathing got better from that very night, and by the next day his eyes were once again showing some signs of life. In ten days or so, he recovered completely and was no longer confined to his bed.

But about the time Yongsul was recovering, it was Oksun this time who became ill. She had, in effect changed places with her son. She had splitting headaches, lost her appetite, had dizzy spells and in all felt so uneasy and suffocated that she could barely endure the pain. People said that the cause of her illness lay in her anxiety at the time of her son's illness, when she often went without eating or sleeping. The consensus was that she would get better were she to recuperate forgetting the world completely.

Hearing news of Oksun's illness, the eldest son of her late husband provided her with a sack of rice and twenty-five gold coins to pay for some medicine.

With the money, Oksun tried everything that was said to be good but none had any effect. Instead, her face got paler by the day and her eyes sank into their sockets.

Also, she started having strange dreams. At first she was having dreams about her dead mother who seemed to call her with gestures of the hands.

But after about a month, an old grey-haired woman, as thin as a rake started appearing in her dreams and took her around mountains, plains, streams and forests. This was during the time when she was supposedly sleeping. So the fatigue when she woke up every morning was agonizing. Her whole body would ache and she felt as if her blood was drying up.

But even during her illness, she could not see her son go without his meals and would come out into the kitchen donning a towel around her head, and barely manage to prepare a bowlful of rice.

It was when this illness had dragged on into its third month. Oksun, reminded of the shrine where she gave prayer when Yongsul had smallpox, decided to visit it again.

'Great spirit, this wretched wench is on the verge of death because of a strange dream. That frightening old woman has been terrorizing me. Please chase the old woman away. If that old woman appears again, I'm sure I'll die. I have no fear about my own death but I cannot leave my Yongsul all alone with no one to look after him. Great spirit, please lend an ear to this wench's wishes.'

After three days of such praying something happened. The old woman who had appeared in her dreams took her around the mountains and fields as she had always done, but this time, she stopped in her tracks for a moment as if she had reached a destination and pointed somewhere saying,

'That's *Jangseunbaeki*.'

Oksun remained, her wits no longer with her.

'It's under the Jangseung (totem pole).'

After uttering these words, she disappeared.

With the apparition gone, Oksun woke up to a severe headache and her whole body soaking with sweat. She was struck by the strangeness of the dream but she could get no hint of what she should do and she passed the day without action. That night the apparition appeared again saying 'That's Jangseungbaeki', 'It's under the Jangseung.'

On the third day, the apparition seemed to have a definitely angrier face. Oksun suddenly felt that she would surely die were she to do nothing again that day. She washed her face and went round to a neighbour to ask where this 'Jangseung-baeki' was and was told that it was the name of a small village in the district of Kyungju. This meant that she would have to travel a good ten kilometres. She set off on the trek. However, on the road itself, Oksun could not help noticing that her steps were surprisingly light.

On arriving at the village, she found the Jangseungs about a kilometre's distance from the nearest house of the village. Originally two Jangseungs had been carved out of one large rock, but now, one had already lost its head and stood in two pieces.

The apparition had not mentioned which Janseung she had meant but Oksun started digging under the headless one in the west. She took out the vegetable knife from her bundle and started scraping at the ground around the pole. She had planned to go and borrow a hoe from the village if the ground proved to be too hard or stony but quite unexpectedly the ground was soft.

When she had dug, perhaps two spans deep in the north western side, a piece of black cloth revealed itself. Digging a little deeper, she discovered it was a kerchief tied as a small bundle, and it seemed certain that there was something inside. Oksun's arms were starting to feel the effects of the exertion and her whole arm was stiff and painful, but having come this far she was not willing to give in. At length, she succeeded in digging it out.

The kerchief had decayed in the earth and crumbled at touch. Oksun somehow managed to pull it out of the ground. The cloth had worn so thin that even before she could untie the knot, it crumbled away leaving a square blue stone container about a span wide all round.

The lid of the box seemed tightly sealed as if glue had been applied all round its edges. Oksun scraped at the joint with the edge of the knife. Inside was something wrapped in a piece of white paper. Oksun started unfolding the paper, her hands shaking. It revealed a bronze mirror, a pair of jade rings, and a small bell.

As these objects lay in front of her, she suddenly felt faint, her heart beating faster, her arms numb and could feel as if the ground would collapse under her feet or the mountain tumble down on its own or some great disaster happen. Her premonitions were unpleasant but by then she had given herself up to whatever would happen, and picked up the mirror and placed it in front of her face. Though the mirror had gathered moss and rust with the passing of time, still, Oksun could recognize that the face which was reflected through the dirt was not her own. It was instead, that of an old woman, the high cheek bones jutting out, the hair dishevelled like the nest of some untidy bird, and the eyes sank a long way into the sockets.

Thinking how strange it all was, Oksun turned the mirror over to study the back. On the top were engravings of what seemed to be Sundo mountain, together with those of the sun and the moon. A little below it were some Chinese characters mentioning something about the illumination of the sun and the moon and the stars, and on either side, in smaller letters, 'The goddess of Sundo' and 'Great goddess'. Of course, she did not have a clue as to their meaning. Indeed, for a long time afterwards, she could meet no one who could adequately explain to her what these letters meant. She had only heard that 'The Goddess of Sundo' signified the female, and was a symbol for 'Sundo' mountain.

Oksun put these objects back into the container and put the lid on, and then wrapped it in her kerchief together with the vegetable knife. She then buried the remains of the black kerchief and covered it with earth.

When Oksun arrived back home, it was about an hour after dusk had fallen. Yongsul lay sleeping in a corner of the ill-lit room. Hiding the container in one corner of the chest, she went out into the kitchen to prepare supper. She herself was of course hungry but more than than, she could not let her son go to sleep without having eaten.

That night, before Oksun had hardly cleared up after supper, she fell fast asleep, exhausted. But about an hour after falling asleep, she was awoken by a nightmare. All through the night she was startled awake, talking in her sleep. It was the same story the next day. Dawn that day, Oksun went back to the shrine.

'Dear spirit, ever since the day I brought the mirror from Jangseungbaeki this wench has been having nightmares talking in her sleep and waking up frightened to death. I don't think I could continue living if this thing goes on any longer. Please may I go and get rid of the mirror. I would not regret my death but how can I leave poor Yongsul on his own. Oh, spirit, please look kindly upon this wretch.'

As she implored the spirit, she bowed continuously. At about the twelfth bow, a voice was heard saying, 'Go to Pakji.' Oksun did not waste a second in going to her. Oksun explained everything that had happened to her up till then. After listening to her, Pakji nodded her head as if she had expected it all along.

'I had a feeling there was something going on between you and me.'

Before these happenings Oksun had heard that a shaman called Pakji lived in the village but it wasn't as if she had heard a lot of her let alone given thought to her. But here she was, twice told by the Spirit at the shrine to go to her. The circumstances were such that she could not deny that some strange turn of fate had tied them together in the past.

'It seems so. Please help me.'

Oksun moved closer to Pakji, dropping her head.

Pakji patted her companion on the back comforting her.

'It seems I've got a spirit daughter.'

Oksun had never heard of the term 'spirit daughter', but assumed it meant 'daughter'. Then tears began flowing down her cheeks. She remembered how her dead mother would not even allow her to serve drinks in the tavern, and now she had fallen so low as to become a shaman. But at the same time, she was overcome by a feeling of security now that she had come to stay with someone who could give her protection.

Pakji dried Oksun's tears with the edge of one of her sleeves.

'Come on, let's get up and go.'

While Oksun used the honorific form of address towards Pakji, Pakji herself used the familiar form. The two women got up and went to Oksun's house.

Oksun sent Yongsul out to the vegetable patch to pick some lettuce and produced the container she had hidden in the chest. Seeing the mirror, the jade rings and the bell, Pakji said, 'An old shaman has sought and found her daughter.'

At last the mystery was solved. It also meant that an initiation ceremony would have to be held. It was decided that the day of the full moon of that lunar month would be the proper date. Full moon was only three days away.

Oksun felt guilty towards her mother and also to the house of her late husband, but on the other hand this was not a matter for her to take round consulting so that there was nowhere from which she could get the expenses for the ceremony. She had no choice but to beg Pakji.

'Could you take charge of everything? I'll repay all when I can.'

Pakji wasn't going to refuse.

41

'If that's how it is, that'll have to do. After all, how can you raise a daughter without costs.'

The place for the ceremony, considering the costs, was to be Oksun's house. The ceremonial table was the same as that provided for the exorcism for Yongsul. But Pakji had to pay for a costume and this was not inexpensive. Pakji had thus taken on quite a burden.

The rush mat had been spread out, the table had been prepared, and next to the table was a smaller stand with a suit of ceremonial dress on top. Pakji sat holding the hour-glass drum in front of the table and Oksun sat on her knees dressed in white in front of the stand with the costume. The initiation ceremony was about to begin in earnest. It was then that Yongsul returned from the vegetable patch.

'Mummy!'

Yongsul had been sent out into the vegetable patch so that he would not have to witness the ceremony, but apparently the sound of the drum had brought him back.

Oksun herself knew that it would be of little use trying to explain things to a four year old child. She waved her arm telling him to leave and Pakji also gave a swish of the drumstick but to no avail. It would be impossible to stop the ceremony to chase a child out and Yongsul was left alone crouching next to his mother.

As the ceremony was nearing its end, villagers crowded around the spectacle. Oksun had long since forgotten the word dignity, but once she was surrounded by spectators her face blushed for yet another time.

'She is not yet fully possessed with a spirit. They say that someone who's possessed cannot feel shame . . .'

These words floated into her ears.

Pakji on the other hand seemed to relish the attention. With more fervour than before, she started chanting the date of birth and the origins of Oksun.

. . . I may not be fully possessed with a spirit . . .

As these thoughts flickered across Oksun's mind, the high pitched voice of Pakji pricked her ears.

'Oh great goddess!'

Oksun was startled for a second. Pakji continued.

'Yes, yes, great goddess, grandmother, grandmother of Sundo mountain. Everything is you great goddess! Yes, grandmother, twice you descended from Sundo mountain to the shrine at Eulhwa-gol and sent our Oksun to Pakji here. Great goddess I worship you.'

After chanting the incantation to the great goddess of Sundo mountain, Pakji brought her hands together. Then picking up the shaman costume from the stand, she threw the clothes to Oksun telling her to change into them.

Oksun put on the yellow jacket on top of the white dress she was wearing, and on top wore the indigo waistcoat.

The people gasped when they saw how beautiful Oksun looked in the shaman costume. Her figure was attractive and her face was captivating. One said she looked like an angel while others said she looked like a *Kisaeng* girl.

Oksun bowed twice towards the ceremonial table as Pakji instructed. Pakji then started to dance holding one of Oksun's sleeves.

'I have a fine daughter, a fine spirit daughter. The goddess of Sundo mountain is going to look after you, look over you and see you safe and help you for years to come.'

The spectators also seemed satisfied, grinning and beaming with pleasure. Oksun was not dancing properly on her own but with Pakji dancing up and down with one of her sleeves in her hand, Oksun was merely trying to keep up steps. But in the process, she was making little dancing movements. And as she did, the ends of her waistcoat flapped delightfully in the wind.

That night Pakji spent the night at Oksun's house.

*Here, 'Guest' refers to the spirit believed to cause smallpox.

Chapter Four
UNDER THE MOONLIGHT

Oksun's house was a small thatched-roofed one with two rooms and a kitchen. But with only Yongsul and herself to house, this meant that the small room was not used as a living quarter. It was used instead to store the pots of rice and other grains, together with unused clothing.

When she was told by Pakji that she had to set up a shrine in her own house, she at first thought of converting the large room. But not knowing what little Yongsul might do, she decided to clear out the small one.

Though the shrine was such in name, not all the formalities could be provided for immediately. She had to be satisfied with a small stand with the stone container on top and a piece of un-dyed cloth serving as the curtain.

Oksun's guardian spirit was to be the goddess of Sundo mountain, otherwise known as the grandmother of Sundo mountain. It was this spirit that had entered her in the initiation ceremony.

For some time after her initiation, Oksun had to live relying on Pakji, working as her helper. There was, of course the need to learn the tricks of the trade from someone who was her senior and who knew the ropes. But more than this, she felt that Pakji should act as a bridge connecting her with her guardian spirit.

Because Oksun regarded Pakji as her spirit mother and because Oksun would be her hands and feet in all matters,

Pakji never hesitated or held back from giving everything she knew to her newly acquired daughter.

'You can't imagine how glad and secure I feel, now that I have Eulhwa with me.'

She would say this regardless of whether Eulhwa was with her or not. Pakji always called Oksun, Eulhwa. It was presumably because the shrine at Eulhwa-gol was the place where the great spirit first descended upon Oksun. As Pakji took Eulhwa around, the rituals she conducted were celebrated for their effectiveness, and the two never failed to attract a sizeable audience wherever they went. On these occasions Pakji would push out her dark pock-marked face and show off her new daughter.

'My daughter's lovely complexion was given by the spirits to make up for my ugly pock-marked face.'

Eulhwa was by nature not the sort of person who ever worried about where her next meal was coming from. Her in-born philosophy seemed to be that a live human being would never gather dust in his mouth, whatever may happen. Perhaps due to this, Eulhwa never expected any reward she could call her own, despite the swelling of the income from Pakji's rituals which were rising in popularity by the minute. She accepted whatever she was given, be it rice or mixed cereal, and was content just to live on without going hungry. In the same way, when Eulhwa went to perform small ceremonies on her own and received small sums of money or grain as her fee, she would give everything to Pakji. Pakji was not by nature very conscious of money nor was she miserly in her attitude, but she seemed to have no qualms about pocketing everything she was given.

Then gradually, the rumour began floating about that Eulhwa's exorcisms would bring miraculous results. This had all started with a small exorcism ceremony Eulhwa had conducted for an eight year old boy in the village. The boy, an only son, suddenly lost the use of one leg without any apparent cause. He would have difficulty in standing up and even more so in walking. All the conventional remedies of medicine and acupuncture had been tried without success. It was then that Eulhwa came and cured the boy with a simple ceremony. Also, another rumour had it that Eulhwa had saved an old man in the neighbouring village from death, suffering from a mysterious illness, and this with an equally simple ceremony.

Upon hearing these rumours, Pakji would say calmly, 'My daughter has at last become a fully fledged herald of the goddess of Sundo.'

The situation having arrived at this, people began demanding Eulhwa's exorcisms more than they did Pakji's. But still, Eulhwa would never accept an assignment without Pakji's permission so that the only way people could get Eulhwa's services was through Pakji. One day Pakji spoke to her on the matter.

'How long do you need me to carry you? From now on, you may take charge of your own rituals without having to get my permission. Our goddess is going to look over you in any case, isn't she?'

Although Eulhwa's exorcisms had brought much miraculous results, she still bore the marks of a tyro, her dance being inexpert, and she was still not able to chant the incantations without obvious pauses. But to compensate, she would invoke the goddess for help with great fervour, performing an unusually large number of bows. She was, in effect, making up for her beginner's clumsiness with faith and devotion.

Be that as it may, as the burden fell more and more on Eulhwa's shoulders, the need for someone to look after the tools of her trade became urgent. The drum, gong, and the fiddle were usually held in a large crate, and someone was needed to carry it around. Up till then she had received the services of Pakji's young helper, but this was only possible when Pakji had no exorcisms of her own, or when the exorcisms she was conducting were so small that she only required her husband, who acted as her head helper.

About this time, there happened to be a very important ceremony in Angang. This required Eulhwa and the whole of Pakji's entourage to go. The crate containing the implements needed in the ceremony was loaded on top of an A-frame together with the ceremonial dress. The procession was led by young master Sung, Pakji's young helper carrying the A-frame on his back, and was followed by Eulhwa, behind whom came Pakji and her husband waving the fan bearing the emblem of the Taekeuk.

Eulhwa spoke to young master Sung.

'Isn't it too heavy? I could carry something if you like.'

No, it's alright. It's better to carry things on one's back anyway.'

Their conversation was simple and functional to the extreme, but it served to hint at their fondness for each other.

That night, finishing the part of the ritual in which the ancestral spirits were beckoned forth out into the open, there remained the ritual in which the spirits had to be sent into the Afterworld to rest in peace. But by some mischievous turn of fate, Pakji was suddenly attacked with cramp in her legs. Pakji and her hosts were in quite a predicament with less than a half of the ceremony completed, and everyone seemed to be uneasy and agitated. It was then that Pakji called on Eulhwa.

'This must be a sign from the goddess herself. She wants you. Go out there and finish the ceremony for me.'

'Don't worry mother. I know I am clumsy at what I do, but I know that our goddess will always be behind me.'

Eulhwa accepted without any hestitation. By luck she knew by heart the incantation for the latter half of the exorcism. In fact, she had for some time felt confident of conducting the banishment ritual but had not had the opportunity till then.

When Eulhwa appeared before the ceremonial table carrying Pakji's fan, she caught the eyes of everyone there who turned in amazement.

There was, of course, the relief that the ceremony could be seen to its conclusion, but more than this, there were the feelings of astonishment and admiration for this charming sorceress, barely twenty years old, with her flower-like face and well formed body captivating everyone with her bewitching movements. Eulhwa at length began the incantation.

'Look at that envoy from the Afterworld.

He has not been able to get what he came for . . .'

Eulhwa enthralled the whole audience in seconds with her soft, affectionate voice. It had a strange power which seemed able to penetrate deep into the listener's flesh. She continued.

'Looking to my right I can see my parents and my brothers and sisters

But who can go instead of me?

Looking to my left there are my wife and my many children

But who can go instead of me?

Looking down I can see my relations

But who cares about me anyway?

As she mixed in a little humour speeding up the tempo of the incantation a little, the audience gave a burst of laughter as they were captivated anew.

She thus made the audience laugh in the beckoning rite, but later in the banishment ceremony she drowned everyone in their own tears. People there were full of praise saying, 'I've never seen a shaman like that,' or 'I can't tell if she's a sorceress or an angel.'

The ritual that night was a huge success, bigger than any that Pakji had seen. The clear, poignant voice together with the peculiar accent and the soft and yet firm voice all combined to get the unconditional admiration of all who were present. But one particular thing which collected the most praise was her masterly technique in the variation of her tempo. She seemed to be gifted from birth with the ability to quicken her speech and glide over the more witty, lighter parts and then to slow down at the serious, emotive parts, attaining the maximum effect.

It was after the first cock crow when the ceremony ended, but Pakji's condition had not improved sufficiently for her to travel so that she and her husband decided to stay on, while sending Eulhwa and young master Sung home to look after the young Yongsul.

As the two passed through the outskirts of the village and out into the stream, the moon of the twelfth day of the lunar month was exceptionally bright. Eulhwa had always been madly attracted by the moon and that night too, she could feel her fatigue being washed away by the moonbeams.

They forded the shallow, gentle stream, crossed the sand, and were following the edge of the forest. Eulhwa suggested they rest for a while. Young master Sung obliged without a reply and stood the A-frame on the edge of the forest.

Eulhwa seated herself on the sand and spoke to her companion.

'Ever since I was a young girl, I've been madly attracted by the moon.'

Young master Sung looked up and struck the same chord.

'Yes, who wouldn't like the moon?'

'A little while back when we were at the stream, I felt all my tired feelings disappear, washed away by the moonlight.'

She stretched her legs and started tapping her legs lightly, massaging them.

'What you did today was no ordinary feat. Doing the banishment ceremony and doing it so well . . .'

He moved closer to her.

'Shall I rub your legs for you?'

He began to massage the lower part of her legs with the wide hands of his.

'How does that feel?'

'That's very refreshing.'

He was encouraged by her reply. He was fearing that she might reproach him for touching her without waiting for an answer in the affirmative. His hands moved up past the knee. Then higher, up to the thighs. Eulhwa let out a moan.

'Ahh . . .'

More excited, his hands went higher, past the thighs, and higher still.

'No, you really shouldn't . . .'

Eulhwa twisted her body and let out a moan. Young master Sung placed his hands under Eulhwa's arms. She undid the ribbon of her *jogori* and revealed her snow-white breasts. She spoke again in a trembling voice.

'I shouldn't . . .'

But young master Sung had already covered the tempting breasts with his hands. He spoke to her as if asking for the final hint.

'I don't know if this is right . . .'

Eulhwa's reply was soon in coming. She said in her trembling, low voice.

'Why not?'

Young master Sung looked round, his hands still grasping her breasts. Nobody was there. But then, that was only natural since it was the middle of the night, nearly dawn. But the moon seemed to be too bright for young master Sung's comfort, and he hesitated. Sensing he might pull away, Eulhwa grabbed hold of one of his sleeves. Master Sung pointed to the forest with his chin.

'There must be softer beds of sand in the forest . . .'

The two entered the forest in each other's arms.

Chapter Five
EULHWA THE SHAMAN

The news of Eulhwa's banishment ceremony was spread by mouth to every part of the county. This news also travelled as far as to reach the house of Master Chung, a local dignitary living within the township of Kyungju, outside the West Gate. The eldest daughter-in-law of that family had her parents' home in Angang and it was her mother who had spoken of Eulhwa to her and through her it had reached the ears of Master Chung's household.

The line of the Chungs was of noble origin and for the last three generations, the household was renowned for its wealth. They owned thousands of acres of rice field which produced a great amount of rice. And it was the lady of the house, Master Chung's mother who was an ardent believer in the effects of shamanistic rituals. So it was that not only at times when someone was ill or dead, but also twice every lunar month, the local shamans would be regularly called on to perform the so called 'invocation' ceremony.

Fortuitously, it happened that the eldest grandson of the household had taken ill some time before then, and was confined to his bed. The local shamans were brought in to perform exorcisms but they had brought no noticeable effect, and the lady of the house was searching for a shaman who could bring home to them some results. When the story of Eulhwa reached her ear, she inquired if Eulhwa could be brought to her.

On her mother-in-law's request the eldest daughter-in-law made haste to Angang. Upon learning of the wishes of the Chung household, the mother of the eldest daughter-in-law took to the road herself and headed to Jatshil with her daughter in front of her.

There was no difficulty in locating Eulhwa's house but getting her consent was another matter. At first, she seemed to have qualms about cutting in when there was apparently another local shaman who tended them.

'It seems there is another daughter of the spirits employed there . . .'

At this rather negative response from Eulhwa, the mother pleaded with her.

'It's the saving of a life that's important. There may be someone who looks after things, but the question of who is employed regularly is a matter of choice.'

At this entreaty, Eulhwa dragged in Pakji as an excuse.

'I do whatever my spirit mother tells me to do.'

'But the lady of the Chung household insists on seeing you.'

'I'm sorry but I can't go anywhere without my mother's consent.'

Eulhwa wouldn't be budged on the matter.

With no choice left to them, the mother and daughter went and besought Pakji. Pakji herself was a little disappointed to learn that it was not her that was called to bring Eulhwa, but thinking it the will of the goddess of Sundo, she resigned herself to Fate and sent young sorcerer Sung equipped with the gong and the drum to Eulhwa.

Though not with relish, Pakji felt that she had an obligation to help Eulhwa by sending young sorcerer Sung with the implements, for this was the least she could do even if she was not in a position to refuse.

From there the daughter-in-law and her mother went straight back to Eulhwa. Seeing that Pakji had even sent along young sorcerer Sung, Eulhwa had no choice but to get dressed and make preparations without further ado. Getting on the carriage at Angang carriage post, they arrived in Kyungju in the evening.

The lady of the house had been expecting her daughter-in-law to bring a new shaman, and it only required the pounding of the rice that had been left soaking in the water to steam some rice cake and for the ceremonial table to be set before the ceremony could begin. The ritual was not the difficult 'banishment' ceremony but the simpler 'beckoning' ceremony, and it was concluded by eleven.

As Eulhwa and young sorcerer Sung were packing up the crates they had brought, the lady of the house came and inquired, 'How did it go? Do you think my grandson has any hope?'

Eulhwa replied, 'Take a look inside.'

'What, are you telling me to go in?'

She couldn't quite believe what Eulhwa was saying.

Eulhwa repeated wearing a smile, 'Yes, go into the room.'

Only then she understood what Eulhwa had said, she went into her grandson's room without uttering another word. Inside was the boy sitting up.

'Insuk, how do you feel? How are you?'

At this question from his grandmother, the boy spoke with great clarity, 'Granny, I want something to eat.'

With colour coming back to her face, the lady of the house said, 'Yes, yes, of course,' and turning to her daughter-in-law ordered, 'Tell someone to make some rice gruel for Insuk.'

No sooner had she given an order she came running to Eulhwa and said in excitement, 'Please, could I see you for a moment?'

Eulhwa was taken into the inner guest room where she was asked quite abruptly, 'Spend the night here.'

'No, I can't. I have a four-year-old child at home alone.'

'Oh, really? Then that's out of the question.'

Then, after a moment's pause, Eulhwa was asked again.

'I do have something to discuss with you quietly.'

'Can't we talk here?'

'Alright, let us do that.'

But then changing the subject again she said, 'Oh, yes, our grandson is up again.'

Eulhwa, as if she had expected it all along said, 'Don't feed him too much at first.'

'Of course.'

Giving this reply, she grabbed Eulhwa by the wrist and pulled her closer to her and said, 'I've heard a lot about you from my daughter-in-law, and I know what a difficult position you're in. I will provide you with a complete set of implements and a fan and costume and enough money – a thousand gold coins – to live on, if only you can come twice a month on the first and fifteenth day of each month for the invocation ceremony and take care of exorcisms for us. For the larger banishment ceremonies, I will reward you separately. How is that? Will you promise?'

Eulhwa, a little flustered, hesitated for a minute and said, 'Those things are too much for me. Also, I cannot do these things on my own.'

'I have heard that you have a spirit mother. If she gives permission, will you accept the offer and promise?'

'Yes.'

'Be that as it may but for the time being, please accept this for tonight's service.'

The lady of the house pressed a green paper bill into her hand. The bill was a ten won note. Even for the arduous and fatiguing banishment ceremony which almost always lasted through the night and which required the efforts of two shamans and two sorcerers, Eulhwa had regarded ten won a very generous remuneration. Thus to her, this sum of money was something astonishing.

'Why do you give so much?'

'Please accept it. From now on, I'll make sure that you won't regret working for me. Please trust me.'

By the time Eulhwa and young sorcerer Sung left Master Chung's house, it was nearing midnight. The two walked in silence through the pitch darkness of the fourth night of the seventh lunar month.

As they passed the village of Nakwondang, and were following the gentle slope of a path over a hill, it was sorcerer Sung who first suggested to rest for a while. And not long after, he grabbed hold of her wrist. Eulhwa did not resist. Instead, she took the lead as the two moved down the slope into the darkness.

The next day, Eulhwa went to Pakji and produced the ten won note that she had received. Pakji did not hesitate in accepting it and said, 'You have really done an excellent job!'

She also added, 'If you feel you need sorcerer Sung, please ask me for him.'

Apart from the literal meaning of Pakji's words, that sorcerer Sung could help in Eulhwa's ceremonies, Eulhwa could sense another meaning in what Pakji said.

53

'I'm very grateful, mother.'

After sitting in front of Pakji with her head bowed down and her face red with embarrassment, Eulhwa went back home.

The green paper bill that Eulhwa had given to Pakji soon started to bring about some other effects as well. The note had obviously played a vital role in squeezing out Pakji's permission in sending Eulhwa to Master Chung's house when the mother of the eldest daughter-in-law came to see Pakji three days later.

By early winter that year, Eulhwa's stomach had grown conspicuously and all knew with fair certainty that it was Sung Doryong who was the father of the child. But no one thought it strange or outrageous. April next year, Eulhwa gave birth to a girl. Two months prior to that, sorcerer Sung had already moved into Eulhwa's house.

Sending Sung Doryong to Eulhwa's house, Pakji had said, 'I was planning to keep you on all my life as my son and workhand but my daughter is the perfect match for you. I knew that nothing could prevent this from happening. Things having come this far, you go and live at her house. But even when you're there, do as you have always done here. I will expect you to do your duties before I remind them to you.'

With this, she gave him a suit of new clothes and fifteen won. By Sung's 'duties', she had meant the making of good luck charms out of paper flowers, painting pictures and playing the gong at rituals. He had entered into Pakji's services as a workhand but he soon displayed his talents for the work of the shaman's helper and was especially skilful in those things which needed dexterity.

His name was Bangdol. His father had been a painter who would, for twenty-seven days out of a month, trudge around far and wide getting spoonfuls to eat here and there by painting little things for his clients. Whenever he thought he had saved enough for a fare, he would return to his home where he would hang around for a few days and then would disappear like a flash. This carried on until the year Bangdol was sixteen years old, when his father disappeared and never returned.

At first, Bangdol had wanted to follow his father's footstep and to become a painter, but his widowed mother, worrying

54

that he would end up like his father, besought him not to do so. After giving up painting, he farmed a patch of land with his mother, but as his mother also died when he was nineteen, he entered someone's house as a workhand. He served there for two years.

One day when he was watching the exorcism performed by Pakji, he suddenly felt envious of the sorcerer Hwarang, who was making paper flowers and painting pictures and beating the gong. Then and there he decided to work for Pakji as a workhand.

He was a good man by nature and besides loving his own daughter, he never neglected looking after Yongsul. At the age of eight Yongsul insisted that he be taught how to read and write, and would settle for nothing else, no one knew how hard he tried to get him into the village school house, taking young Yongsul by the hand and begging that he be accepted. But when, on the reason that he was a shaman's son, he was refused entry, Bangdol got hold of the basic textbook containing the thousand characters of Chinese, copied out half the characters by hand and taught Yongsul himself. But Yongsul's capacity for learning characters was extraordinary, and Bangdol himself not having even mastered the thousand letters, he was soon scraping the bottom of the barrel. It broke Bangdol's heart to see such a thing and suggested once to Eulhwa, 'What do you think about sending Yongsul to study in the temple? There, there is no discrimination on grounds of social status.'

Eulhwa happily agreed, and left for Kirim Temple holding Yongsul by the hand, saying she knew a priest there.

The period of two or three years after Eulhwa had sent Yongsul to the temple was probably the happiest in her life. The devoted love of her husband was everywhere, in the running of the house, the exorcisms, and in the bed, and the popularity of her rituals was rising every day, and Wolhie was growing up so beautifully, looking like something carved out of jade and made out of the soul of the moon. It seemed that everything she saw and encountered held some happiness for her.

But even during these blissful months, there were times when she trembled with fear and unease. They usually came after an indulgent night in bed. She would tell her husband

55

shaking with fear that although the goddess of Sundo mountain had at first turned a blind eye to her ever-indulgent sex life now it seemed that she (the goddess) was losing her patience.

One day, while all this was going on, Wolhie suddenly stopped eating and would only live on water. Then, about fifteen days later, her tongue seemed to be retreating into her throat and Wolhie started having difficulties in speaking.

Eulhwa judged that the long awaited punishment from the goddess had at last arrived. From then on, on days when she had no exorcisms to perform, she would go to the shrine at Eulhwa-gol or venture even deeper into the woods to pray and beg forgiveness.

It was also about this time that there came gradual changes in Eulhwa's speech and bearing. Before, she would only be possessed with a spirit after chanting the initial incantation and hearing the gong and the bells, but now, she was continuously and continually hazy, as if she were possessed by some spirit at all times.

It was a bright, moon-lit night. Eulhwa came back home after roaming the mountain gorges and streams all through the night, and as if chanting a spell, she told her husband, 'Our Dahlie (Wolhie) is the seventh princess of a moon god who lived in a palace on the moon. This god had seven daughters and our Dahlie was the youngest. Originally, he had promised the hands of his seven daughters to the seven sons of Emperor Jesuk, the supreme god. The hand of the first daughter was given to the first son, the second to the second son, the third to the third son and so on. But when it came to the matching of the seventh son, the match did not go as planned. The seventh son was a little flirtatious by nature and could not wait his turn and stole the sixth princess. The sixth prince and the seventh princess who had lost their partners asked that they be married, but the prince was taken to the Dragon god in the Underwater and was married to his third daughter, while the seventh princess descended to the land of mortals. It is no wonder that a guest from a foreign land as far as that cannot speak our language fluently.'

Eulhwa would spin this yarn to explain why Wolhie had lost her tongue. And to her husband, she said that though at first Wolhie's loss of speech was a punishment given by the goddess of Sundo mountain for her over-indulgence, she said in passing that she had learned it was otherwise.

From the time Wolhie had difficulty in speaking, Wolhie started painting. Her father Bangdol said that her talent in painting was given to her before birth in a previous life. For Wolhie herself, there were no signs of anxiety or discomfort. Indeed, for her who never went outside to play, there really was no need to be able to speak. As the story invented by Eulhwa had said, Wolhie really did seem like a shy soul from the moon who disliked being surrounded by other people.

It was when Wolhie had reached the age of eight. News came from the lady of Master Chung's house asking Eulhwa to move house into the town. Eulhwa herself was quietly hoping that something of the sort would happen, the reason being that she performed exorcisms mainly to the south of the town and in consequence had to make long journeys of eight kilometres or more and that was certainly not an easy thing to do. She did not accept requests from the north of the township for she wanted to give that part to Pakji. Moving house had been made possible because a suitable house had been found.

The house had originally been used as some kind of shrine or sanctum, and long ago, a pundit of some kind had occupied the house. When this pundit left, a widowed woman who used to take charge of the washing for him remained alone in the house. But some time after, this widow started claiming that being his prime disciple she had received the spirit of the pundit and started fortune-telling. People referred to her variously as 'the old woman of the shrine', Myongdo hag, Taeju hag, and so on. Her fortune-telling was apparently very accurate and the lady of the house of Master Chung had also called her a few times. But later, a weird and horrifying incident had taken place and the hag had been chased away, expelled to a place faraway.

Eulhwa herself was well acquainted with this incident. With the departure of the hag the house was left empty. But no ordinary person could or would live in it. So the only alternative to leaving it empty was to bring someone like Eulhwa to live in it. This was exactly what was requested of her.

Chapter Six

THE RISE OF EULHWA
THE SHAMAN

After moving into the new neighbourhood, the relationship between Eulhwa and Bangdol became more and more estranged.

For a start, there was the house itself. To Eulhwa, everything about the house pleased her, but for Bangdol, he always felt uneasy because to him, it was rather spooky and there seemed to be something which wasn't quite right. The same was true of the attitude of the inhabitants there. Their curious smiles or the uninterested expressions on their faces were to Eulhwa, a sign of good will whereas to Bangdol, they were that of contempt and alienation.

The differences in opinion did not end with these rather trivial emotions. In the actual running of the house, Bangdol was the one who wanted to keep the house spotless, pulling out the weeds in the yard, mending the stone walls in the places which had been damaged, while Eulhwa was just the opposite, only wiping out the dust from the rooms. She claimed that terrible things would be brought about if anything were done to the house. As for pulling the weeds from the yard, she even went as far as to say that it was like pulling or cutting her own hair. Eulhwa was an easy going person on all ordinary matters but when it came to affairs dealing with the spiritual, she was extreme and would cling violently to what she believed was right. For the mild mannered Bangdol for whom arguing or fighting was not in his nature, there was no choice but to follow her assertions.

However, as time went on, things began happening which Bangdol could not allow. It all began when Eulhwa began drinking, and as her habit got worse, there accompanied a myriad of harmful 'side-effects'.

The tavern Eulhwa frequented was a small, insignificant place, known as Mogwajip (the quince tavern), or Sungmitjip (the tavern under the wall). The reason it was called the quince tavern was in the fact that the face of the landlady resembled a quince, and the reason it was called the tavern under the wall was because it lay at the foot of what remained of the old city walls, now a pile of rubble. Eulhwa called the owner 'older sister' while she in turn called Eulhwa 'younger sister'. How they first met or what drove them together to be that close was not known but it was the opinion of all who knew them that they were closer than blood sisters.

It wasn't certain where the quince woman got her yeast and water but the taste of the home brew was so famous that the house was never empty of regular boozers and tipplers, even though the tavern was no more than a wretched hut surrounded by rubble. On days when she had no exorcisms, she would just as well have been living there, with the owner and Eulhwa calling each other sister.

The visitors of the tavern were mainly members of what could be termed as the lower classes, and among them were some helpers of shamans. And in as much as they knew Eulhwa's name, they were all the more polite and generous to her.

Among these, there was a sorcerer aged about forty by the name of Sol, and he showed interest in Eulhwa from the beginning. He started by buying her a few drinks and in no time learned of Eulhwa's position and ended up by suggesting that he help in Eulhwa's ceremonies. The husband of a shaman was almost always her helper, but in big exorcisms one was not really enough. It was customary to hire another helper when conducting these big affairs. What was more, although Bangdol was skilful in making paper flowers and in painting, he was still not at home playing the gong, the various types of drums, fiddle, and other instruments.

The content of Sol's proposition was that he would take charge of playing the drums and fiddle if Bangdol would do the same with the making of the paper flowers and playing the gongs.

Eulhwa was, of course, in favour. Bangdol himself was aware of the necessity of hiring other helpers but he felt uncomfortable about having one of his wife's drinking acquaintances being brought in to help them.

After some time, Bangdol began to realize that the relationship between his wife and this man called Sol was no ordinary professional relationship. There was, in the neighbourhood, a gambling rascal whose nickname was 'longlegs', who was an occasional visitor to the quince tavern, and according to the rumour he had spread, Eulhwa and Sol had a love affair going between them from long ago and their relationship was overtly recognized and accepted by the people at the tavern. But then once when Sol was away helping in an exorcism, another rascal who frequented the tavern, a cattle dealer who incidentally had for a long time held interest in Eulhwa, came to have a liaison with her. In the course of their carrying on, Sol found out about the affair and a violent fight apparently followed.

When Bangdol questioned Eulhwa on the matter, she hid nothing and admitted all, but begged he give her another chance and promised that it would not happen again.

'I wasn't born a bad woman but I must have been out of my senses when I did that. I had too much to drink. But I have never failed in serving you.'

This was her defence. And it was true. In the bed, and in the meal tables she offered up, Bangdol could hardly have asked for more.

But despite the promises she made, she was neither able to stop drinking at the quince tavern nor did she clear up the matter concerning the two men there. Instead, it was left to drag along. The rumours had it that the two were kept from killing each other by the quince woman who somehow got in between them and arranged things in such a way that there was no trouble.

Then all of a sudden, Bangdol left on a journey. Judging from the fact that he had not discussed the journey beforehand there was something out of the ordinary. He came back after about a week and told Eulhwa rather forcefully, 'I think I'll go out to the East Sea coast and mind a small shop. I'm thinking of taking Wolhie with me. What do you think?'

Eulhwa was quite drunk when he spoke to her but on hearing what Bangdol was planning to do, she held his sleeves with both hands and cried, rather, chanted with tears in her voice.

'You're too cruel, too cruel,
My husband, you're too cruel,
You cannot take her, you cannot,
You cannot take our Dalhie,
Our Dalhie will die,
She will die if she leaves me.'

She tried on finishing her chant to embrace him. Bangdol knew that she could not let Wolhie go. He quietly pushed her away and stood up and left. He did not return.

About a month later, Eulhwa heard that Bangdol was keeping a small shop on the east coast selling dried sea food such as dried fish, octopus, and seaweed. Eulhwa was always thinking of visiting him but somehow did not get around to it. Instead Bangdol came with some dried seaweed, perhaps once every season to see his daughter. Even after Bangdol's departure, Eulhwa would always stand him out as her husband. This was especially true when she was with either Sol or the cattle dealer.

Chapter Seven
THE CHURCH IS FOUND

Yongsul began to have some idea of just how far his mother's sentiments and beliefs were from those of Christianity. He also realized how rocky and steep the road would be in making her understand and accept it. The prospect was daunting. But the truth was that his mother was no longer the mild-mannered, perhaps even naive woman he used to know, but was now a completely different person, utterly the possession of some devilish spirit. His once gentle and meek mother, full of compassion was now a short-tempered, violent and stubborn woman.

That time when Yongsul referred to his mother's 'spirit' as an idol, the colour of her face had changed suddenly and she had abused him calling him a demon and an evil spirit. If Yongsul had put up the least bit of resistance, she may well have thrown the water from the water bowl in his face. His mother as he had known her was not the sort of person who could lose her temper and attack someone with any degree of violence. He sighed that in the ten years she had spent as a shaman she had been transformed into a stranger. He had come with his heart full to the brim with the Gospel, but for him to plant his hopes, the ground was too rocky and the sun was too hot.

One of the reasons for his leaving Pyongyang was that he had missed his mother and sister very much, but more than this, he had wanted to share with them by spreading the

Gospel, the almost frightening happiness that he had been able to enjoy. This was his wish and also his objective. He did not think this task would prove too difficult. Indeed, his dream and his ultimate objective, once he had converted his mother and sister, was to disseminate the message to all the inhabitants of the area, found a church, conquer superstition, drive out evil, and lead the people lost in the darkness to the house of light and hope.

However, the road to the fulfilment of his hopes and aspirations was too far and rocky. Even leaving his mother aside, there was the present state of his sister. The charming little girl, as kind-hearted as an angel, and one who would trust and love him to such an extent, was now in the clutch of the same evil spirit that was holding his mother. Indeed, she even seemed to be avoiding him and what was even more lamentable was that she was hardly able to understand what he said. He of course attributed her disability to the work of the devil. But despite the difficulties, he was not going to give up. He reminded himself that the deeper the superstition embedded in the people, the harder he must try to save them from the clutch of the devil.

The only thing which gave him this courage and will was of course his iron faith. He believed firmly that his dreams would surely be realized through his prayers. Indeed, this was the ultimate strength and weapon against which all was powerless and one that he had kept safely in his heart ever since his departure from Pyongyang.

But his immediate problem was finding a place to pray. It was quite out of the question to offer prayers in a house which was full of images of all sorts of demons together with charms and effigies of all kinds. Furthermore, if his mother were to see him, she would no doubt come out with her accusations of him being a devil and demon. But for that matter, he could not simply come out of the house to pray in the yard. There were pictures of demons all around the walls of the house and the weeds made it impossible for him to venture anywhere else.

The next day, he decided to look for the church in the area. He gathered that the only place from where he could receive any strength or consolation was the church.

The church, often called the 'house of worship' in the area

was a low, shed-like building with a tin roof. In the front yard stood a willow, and beside this willow was a bell tower, about twice the height of the main building. It seemed the well was opposite the bell tower. A woman aged around thirty was proceeding towards the well with an empty earthenware jar on her head appearing from behind the church building. Youngsul followed her to the well.

'Excuse me ma'am, but do you think I could have a drink of water?' Yongsul asked politely.

The woman looked at Yongsul, seeming a little flustered, and said, 'Oh dear, there isn't a bowl . . .' and then asked, 'Do you mind drinking from the well bucket?'

Yongsul smiled and replied in his native accent, 'Anything's fine.'

The woman drew a fresh bucketful of water from the well, poured a little off from the top and lifted it in front of Yongsul's face.

'Here you are.'

Yongsul held the bucket with both his hands and drank straight from it. As he poured away what was left down into the gutter and was handing the empty bucket to the woman, a small, scrawny man, aged about forty appeared from behind the church building and approached him. He wore a dirty yellowish western style pair of trousers on top of which he wore a white *jogori* with a dark grey waistcoat on top. On his head was a well-weathered straw hat.

'May I help you?' asked the man as he came closer to Yongsul.

'Hello, I was born and brought up here, and I have just returned from a long stay in Pyongyang. Are you with the church?' Yongsul asked, his head bowed down a little.

By his question, he was asking both whether he was a believer who attended the church and whether he was the caretaker. His experiences told him that every church would have someone who lived behind the main building, taking charge of the cleaning and ringing the bell and so on. Yongsul assumed this man was also such a person.

'Yes, I look after the church. I live right there.'

He pointed to the back of the church. From the accent of the man's speech, Yongsul gathered that he was a native of the area. He was called Deacon Kim.

'This area is my home, but I have been away for a long time. In Pyongyang, I was under the care and love of an American missionary named Hyun Dalsun (Henderson).'

Yongsul readily introduced himself and made his wishes known because he wanted to be able to get the cooperation of Deacon Kim. The response was of warm welcome, full of emotion and he told Yongsul that he could come out to the church anytime he wished and that he would slip in a good word to Mr. Yang Josa, who was in charge of the church.

'How many believers do you have?'

'I don't know for sure, but I think there are more than a hundred because the hall is nearly full on Sundays.'

Kim walked up to the church door as he said this and opened the door. In the hall was a low barrier made of plywood separating it down the middle. He was told that the half to the East was for women and the one to the West, for men. Each compartment seemed to be about seventy or so square yards in area. Compared with some of the large churches he had seen in Pyongyang or Seoul, the facilities were primitive. But to think that a house preaching the Gospel had opened here, his birthplace, the church's existence was a very surprising and gratifying thing.

'The ardent believers turn up round the clock to pray, even on weekdays,' said Kim as if to encourage Yongsul.

Besides this, Kim told Yongsul about the present situation of the church and its attendants as the facts turned up in his head. Among the things he said, the story of a Master Park was particularly encouraging to Yongsul. What he found so interesting was not the fact that he was the founder of the church, of which he was the only elder, or that he looked after the church's affairs as he would his own, coming to visit the church whenever he came within the city walls. Instead, it was the fact that the reason he gave himself to Christianity was apparently to defeat superstition.

'What was he originally?'

'Well, originally, he was one of the noblemen from Bamdul. A very wealthy landlord, too. When the country fell to the Japs, he threw away everything he had, saying that he was ashamed to be a member of the noble class and moved into the town.'

'I would like to meet the gentleman very much.'

'Yes, of course you must. He visits the church every day and on Sundays, it goes without saying.'

Yongsul bowed his head in gratitude and went into the church. The floor was of wood, and high up on the piece of plywood which divided the hall hung lamps in large numbers. The lamps were not lit for it was still before midday but Yongsul did not feel it was particularly dark inside. This was probably because on both the west-facing and east-facing walls were two glass windows each, illuminating the hall.

After looking slowly around the whole room, he sat on his knees in the middle of the hall and closed his eyes. His prayer which started thus lasted for more than two hours.

After offering his prayers, he took out the small copy of the Bible from inside his coat and started reading from the beginning of St. John's Gospel. By the time he had read about twenty pages, it was well past lunch time, but strangely, he did not feel hungry. He left the church and went to the back of the church to Mr. Kim's house.

'Mr. Kim, do you have a rag I could use?'

Hearing Yongsul's voice, Kim opened the door of his room and said, 'You are a very commendable young man.'

'Not at all. You put me to shame.'

Yongsul answered in his own native accent. Without his knowing it, he was using expressions and intonations of his birthplace without any difficulty whatsoever.

'What are you going to do with the rag?'

'I was thinking of washing the windows.'

'Oh, leave it. I'll be doing those tomorrow.'

'No, it's alright. I'll just wash the windows on the men's side of the room.'

When Yongsul almost implored him, Kim gave him a cloth, feigning defeat. For some reason, Yongsul was very thankful when he received the cloth. After cleaning the windows, he returned the rag having washed it spotlessly clean.

The next day too, Yongsul offered his prayers in the empty hall after which he washed the windows on the women's side of the hall.

On the third day, after his usual prayer in the hall, he was planning to sweep the church yard, and was on his way to Kim's house to borrow the broom. By chance, Kim was talking with a rather tall man with a large jet-black moustache grown either side of his face. He wore a white overcoat and seemed very imposing. Seeing Yongsul, Kim gestured him to come nearer.

'Young man, come this way.'

When Yongsul approached him, Kim pointed to the man in the white overcoat and said, 'This is Master Park, the presbyter that I have told you about.'

Yongsul made a deep bow. Master Park twirled the end of his moustache and said, 'So, you have been in Pyongyang, have you?'

'Yes, sir.'

'Under a missionary?'

'Yes, sir.'

'And is this your native town?'

'Yes, sir.'

'And your name?'

Yongsul could not reply and only his face flushed red. He was an illegitimate child and hence he did not have a surname. While he was at the temple, he had used the same of 'Suk', and in Pyongyang under the missionary, he had used the surname of the missionary himself, 'Hyun'. But now, in front of Master Park he could not bring himself to use either Suk or Hyun. After some hesitation, he barely managed to use his mother's surname and said his name was Bae Yongsul.

'Where is your house?'

Yongsul was again lost for an answer. He was afraid that if he told him he lived in the Sungbak area, his identity as the shaman's son would be exposed. He answered, with a voice like that of a mouse, 'It's in the Sungbak area.'

'You mean Soburi?'

'Yes, sir.'

'The you're in the same neighbourhood as I am. What, if I may ask, is your father's name?'

'He's not with us.'

'Did he pass away?'

'Yes, sir.'

'Oh dear, tut tut,' and continued, 'If you have nothing more to do, perhaps you would like to walk home with me.'

It was no ordinary show of hospitality and good will for a church elder like Master Park to ask a young man he hardly knew to walk home with him.

67

But Yongsul could not answer straight away. He guessed that while walking together he would be asked in detail about his background and it was almost certain that his identity would be revealed. But the next moment, recalling that he would have to receive his help and guidance in any case, he thought it could prove to be a good opportunity. He reaffirmed his will to confess that he was a shaman's son and the fact that he was a bastard, and answered, 'Yes sir, but it's too great an honour . . .'

'Not at all. It's time our church had young men like you.'

He seemed to be stating his own view of the future role of the church.

When they reached the entrance of the neighbourhood, Master Park stopped in his tracks and asked, 'Where is your house?'

Yongsul pointed towards the centre of the neighbourhood and said in his native accent, 'It's over there,' and continued, this time in the standard Seoul accent, 'Sir, I have something to talk over with you. When will you have time?'

'Really? Any time will do. Right now if you wish. Come with me. Let's discuss it over supper, perhaps.'

Park thus agreed without any qualms whatsoever.

Presbyter Park's house was sited at the edge of a field on the eastern end of the Sungbak neighbourhood. The nameplate read, 'Park Kunshik'. Yongsul was led into the guest room, and despite the master's urges to sit comfortably, remained seated on his knees. After seeing the host take his seat, he got up and offered a deep obeisance and sat as he had done before.

'I have something for which I must beg your forgiveness, sir.'

'What is it? Please tell me.'

Even after getting the master's permission, Yongsul hesitated and finally managed to say, 'I, I am really the son of, of a shaman.'

'What . . . a shaman?'

'Yes, sir, and up to now, I have no idea of who my father is or what he looks like.'

'If your mother is a shaman, then you must be the son of the sorceress who lives . . .'

'Yes, sir.'

'Then it is that house.'

Master Park mumbled to himself seeming very surprised. He lifted his face and after looking Yongsul in the face for some time, readied himself to say something then decided not to.

'It's been four days since I arrived home.'

'Then you wouldn't know the story behind that house . . . Anyway, continue with what you were saying.'

From the way he spoke, there seemed to be something about the house that Master Park knew, but he could not ask what it was straight away. As the master had asked him, Yongsul told of his past as far as he could remember. But still, Yongsul was only ten when he had left home and it was true that he knew little about his life before his departure or of his birth.

'The reason I try to hide my origins is not out of any desire to deceive anyone but simply that if I were to tell the truth, people would not accept me and that is my greatest fear,' added Yongsul.

'There is nothing to fear. In that respect Christianity is a fine religion. As you know, Christ himself dealt mainly with people in such positions as yours.'

After trying to console him thus, he concluded what he was saying with, 'I like youthful and wise young men like you. You could even be the young man I have been waiting for in my heart.'

Gathering courage from what he heard, Yongsul said, 'When I first went to the church, the man called Mr. Kim who looks after the church told me so much about you. Among the things he said, the part which impressed me most was that you became a Christian because of your wish to rid this land of superstition, and I promised myself that I would seek your teaching.'

The master made no reply but nodded his head, after which he said, 'You are right. The reason lies in the house you are living in now,' and looked at Yongsul with eyes that had taken on a new fire.

'Our house, sir?

'Yes.'

He replied softly and proceeded to tell the story of his conversion to Christianity.

Chapter Eight
ELDER PARK

As Deacon Kim had said the Elder Park Kunshik was indeed the most eminent person in his family, the Chestnut Plain Parks. The Chestnut Plain Parks had for three generations produced men who had passed the first round of the State Civil Service Examinations and had thus earned the title of 'Chinsa' or 'Scholar'. For five generations it had also boasted enough wealth to produce a thousand sacks of rice at harvest time. They were country nobility and they owned land. The three generations of 'Chinsa' went down as far as his grandfather's, and the money had lasted to his generation.

He forsook this ancient lineage and left for Soburi the year after the country was annexed by the Japanese. At this time he was thirty-five. So, at thirty-four when he heard the shocking and tragic news, he cried:

'If one has lost one's country what matters it whether one is commoner or noble? Of what use is my topknot?[1]'

And he cut off his topknot with his own hands and offered to his ancestral shrine and for three days did not cease his lamentations. Three days later he came out of the ancestral shrine and prostrated before his father and did not rise. He said:

'Please grant this unfilial wretch permission to leave thy side.'

When his father heard that Kunshik had cut off his topknot without permission at first he could not contain his anger and

70

jumped up and down with rage. But when Kunshik, after having lamented for three days, came out of the shrine and prostrated himself asking permission to leave for far-off parts, he was so amazed that he could say nothing and just sat there sucking the stem of his bamboo pipe. When a whole day had passed with no results, the son still prostrating himself at his father's feet and the father still sucking wordlessly at his pipe, his mother could no longer bear to watch and pleaded with his father asking if he would be satisfied with no less than seeing his son die. This hard-won permission consisted of nothing more than the words: 'Get up and get out of my sight.'

So the son who had 'gotten out of his father's sight' went to his room and collapsed and did not rise until nine days later. Even this he would not have done had it not been for his mother's words: 'If you die there shall be no one left in our house.'

Having summoned his son, now up and about the old man started to remonstrate with him:

'So, where will you go if you leave my side?'

'Father, please forgive me. I dare not open my eyes to look at the sun and the moon in the sky for shame.'

'Are you the only one to have lost his country? Will the country be regained by your single death? Why is it that you think that your life belongs to you and to you alone? If you go off what shall become of us?'

Even as the old man said these words, he did not understand what was meant by 'going off'. With his head still bowed the son did not answer.

'At least you can give me a satisfactory answer. Where do you intend to go?'

'Father, please forgive me. I would like to shave my head and enter the mountains.'

'What? Become a monk?'

Kunshik remained silent.

'To become a monk is the same as disappearing from the face of this earth. You do not deserve to be called a man. How can you be so cold-hearted? So you will forsake your aged father and mother, your poor wife and children to set off alone to do this monk business? Why you barbarian dog!'

So the old man cried in a voice like thunder and fell sick and took to his bed. And from that day on it was the old man's turn to refuse all food and drink. His wife would prepare gruel and beg him to eat, all to no avail.

'I shall die before I see that brat go about doing his monk business.'

Hearing these words the wife went to plead with her son. Weeping and grasping her son, she cried:

'Must you see your father dead and buried? Please please, at least tell him that you will not lead the life of a wandering monk.'

Day and night she clung to him and wept. As if he could no longer bear it, the son at last went to his father and begged him to get up and break his fast, for he would forsake the idea of going about as a wandering monk.

Next spring, the son again prostrated himself before his father.

'What is it?'

'Father, this worthless brat would like to move to town and begin the work of regaining our country. Please I beg you to grant your permission.'

'Regain our country?'

'Yes.'

His voice was full of steadfast determination. After thinking for a long while, the old man said:

'I hate unto death the idea of your leaving this house but is that not at least better than going about on this monk business. Though you live away from home let you come home often, in all matters large or small concerning the family to say nothing of birth, death and marriage and rites.'

So under this condition did he grant his permission. Kunshik entrusted family matters to his brother and found a house in the town. He had wanted to move in with his wife and family, but his father forbade this, saying:

'Let you go alone and leave your wife and children here. If that is inconvenient you may install a concubine there, but you may not take your wife and children with you.'

'Father, to lead that dissolute life would this worthless brat forsake his parents and leave this roof? Everyone knows about so-and-so of Chestnut Plain. With matters as they are what would people say if I too were to go around with a concubine?'

'Though you be reduced to cooking your own rice, your wife stays here. You may not take her with you before I die.'

72

And his father remained resolute to the end. Since he could do nothing else, Park Kunshik was forced to take just the Kims, a couple who had until now looked after the running of the house. Perhaps a month had passed when his mother came to see him in town and said:

'However many times I talked things over with your father I find there is little else we can do. At such an age how can you live alone, and that not just for a couple of days. Your wife and children must stay at Chestnut Plain. Both your father and I, we must soon leave this world. Since you who are the master of the Park clan are living out like this, though the sky may crack and split into two your wife and children must remain at Chestnut Plain. So . . .'

She broke off and looked at her son. Kunshik could vaguely guess what his mother was trying to say.

'Mother, my younger brother can take care of Chestnut Plain.'

'There are matters you can leave to your brother and this is not one of them. The eldest son must be responsible for the clan. You are the head of the Park clan. Your father still bitterly regrets the day when he let you leave for town, and so he says that though the sky may crack and split into two pieces he will not let your wife and children go. So no more talk, and bring a gentle girl as concubine. Your wife's uncle told me of a meek and well-brought up girl at the Dwitshil village and so I went to see. Though she is past marrying age she is only twenty and such a fine girl you could not find. If she was any ordinary girl do you think your wife's uncle would have rushed over to tell me?'

'Mother, can you not feel what is in my heart?'

'No, it is not because I don't see how you feel. Who does not feel grief for having lost one's country? But you cannot put matters of State to right by yourself and matters of our clan depend utterly on you, do they not? Though it be sinning before your ancestors and unfilial to your parents if it were something you could put to right by yourself, would we, though we are parents, try to restrain you?'

And even Kunshik could say nothing upon such words of his mother.

'If you don't want to go all the way to Dwitshil village I shall take care of matters myself. Though you may come to be Lord of all under heaven you must first put out the fire at your ankles.'

A fortnight or so after this, his mother came to town with this twenty-year-old maid.

Though he knew in his heart of hearts that this matter was in no way meet nor fitting he did not wish to enter into conflict with his parents again, and there was the need to supply what his body craved for. So he met the guest under the pretence of giving way to his parents' wishes.

Upon understanding that Kunshik had decided to take the woman as concubine, his father summoned and gave him five hundred won and said in a more pacified voice.

'This is what is left of the money that I had saved to buy land. You took five hundred won to buy your house and this is what is left. Take it and use it as you see fit, whether you choose to spend it on starting a business or to save the country, but don't think of selling our land to get more money.'

'Father, I have no intention of spending the money on gambling or whoring. But how can I save the country with five hundred won?'

'It is not that I don't know your feelings. But you must guard the clan. Without family there can be no country.'

Since he could not very well fight with his father, on that day he just took the money and went back to town.

When he arrived back in town, he was told that someone from the Choi family in the neighbouring village had dropped in. The Choi's were prominent among the various noble families in the district and Choi Kam, the head of the clan, was someone he had respected and revered for a long time. There he was introduced by Choi Kam to a man from Seoul named Ahn Hyuk. Ahn said he was here on secret orders from Rhee Syngman to raise funds in order to gather resistance fighters. Choi Kam gave five hundred won as funds and urged Park to do his utmost to help. Park was delighted with his suggestions and gave three hundred won on the spot.

Afterwards he used what was left, which was less than one hundred won on a trip to Seoul. After having seen how things were in the capital he went down back home and reported to Choi Kam. There were kin living in Seoul, but since Choi had asked him to see some people there, he had to report to Choi as quickly as possible. After hearing the news Choi asked, stroking his beard.

'Well, did you find out about the resistance fighters?'

He talked down to Park Kunshik, since he was fifteen years the elder and was someone who Park had respected and revered since childhood, and was besides his village elder.

'It is true that Ahn Hyuk is involved in matters of resistance but he says that we cannot save the country by selling off our estates for military funds.'

Choi Kam retorted as if to tell him off.

'Who does not know that? We are doing this because it is at least better than sitting around doing nothing.'

'That is true, sir. What Ahn Hyuk suggested was to use the funds for a more farsighted project, that is to say to set up a school or to send students abroad.'

Choi said nothing and pondered for a long time with his head bowed, then slowly raised his head and said in a low voice.

'That is right.'

Since at that time the country was still under military government, education establishments could not be readily set up, and it was no easy matter to get hold of so much funds. Hence, Choi took the job of getting in touch with the Japanese authorities and buying the lot on which the school would be built and Park took responsibility for the school building and the hiring of teachers.

Park Kunshik went back to Chestnut Plain to see his father and again begged him to sell off the land which was worth five hundred sacks of rice yearly and which by rights belonged to Kunshik.

'What will you do with the money?' asked the old man abruptly.

'I wish to spend it on educational work.'

'I can guess what you are driving at, but I cannot permit that. If you must do so do it after I am dead. That land is what received my ancestors. How can I sell it off as I like?'

'Father, what use is land when we no longer have a country?'

'Ancestors do not disappear because the country is no more. Even if a State is gone our ancestors remain. Rather would I die than commit a crime against my ancestors.'

75

Having laid down the law he sat with his back facing Kunshik as if to say 'I am not listening to any more of what you say.'

Since it was useless to fight with his father when he was like that, Kunshik went back to town.

Not six days after he had left, he received the sudden news that his father had taken ill. When he rushed over to Chestnut Plain he was told that his father had taken to bed soon after Kunshik's departure and had neither been able to sleep nor to eat at all well and could not get up and move about. They had called in many doctors, but they had not even been able to properly diagnose the illness nor had medicines been of any avail. The general conclusion was that he had received a violent shock from the argument with his son that day.

Fearful that his father was still worried about the land Kunshik tried to reassure him.

'Father, please ignore what this worthless brat has said about the educational work and please do not worry about it. Scholar Choi has agreed to take care of it and I have agreed to just run errands for him.'

At first his father said nothing. A long time afterwards he asked in a low and reproachful voice.

'Do you mean you shall be someone's errand boy?' His eyes gleamed with light.

'No, sir. It does not mean I shall be an errand boy. It will be to serve and help a good elder like Scholar Choi.'

His father said nothing and just shook his head. He turned and lay on his side, his back facing Kunshik.

Perhaps a fortnight later Kunshik received the news that his father was in critical condition and raced over to Chestnut Plain. When he saw his son the old man said, his eyes gleaming.

'Of the seven hundred "sok" of land, that is in your name, five hundred belongs to our family and not to you personally. So even if I die do not touch a single grain of rice on that land. If I live, I live to see myself committing a crime against my ancestors so I would rather die in a hurry and escape that. Do not trample on my wishes even though I am not here.'

And he left this last request. Three days later he died.

After his father's death Kunshik locked himself up in the house and did not set foot outside for three months, believing that he alone had caused his father's death. After a year's mourning Kunshik went to town and met Scholar Choi. After he had listened to his story Scholar Choi said:

'Your father's words are right. From olden times it had been said: "There can be no loyalty to the state without filial piety." But I do not say that your desire to regain our country is wrong. I believe that your desire to regain our country is far greater than filial piety or loyalty to the state, since there can be neither filial piety nor loyalty to the state if there is no state. But this does not mean that I ask you to go against your father's will. I am just telling what my frank opinion on the matter is. Let us talk about this again once you have stopped wearing mourning.'

As Scolar Choi advised he gave up all work until the day he would stop wearing mourning, and on the first and fifteenth of every lunar month he went to Chestnut Plain and faithfully guarded his father's tomb.

With less than six months to the day he shed his mourning garb his eldest son who was twelve that year took to bed with an unknown illness. Panic stricken the boy's mother had consulted a fortune-teller who told her that a foul ghost of some sort was haunting the house, and rushed out to town to ask her husband what they should do.

'It's a doctor we need. What does a fortune-teller have to do with it?'

'What else could I do when the doctors could tell me nothing?' She answered him thus and continued.

'In this very neighbourhood lives Granny Taeju so I shall go and find out from her to put my mind at ease.'

Thinking that at least they would lose nothing in doing so Kunshik let her go. But that night when his wife came home, she said: 'That Granny Taeju has disappeared.'

'Where did she go?'

'No one knows. They say she has run off having committed some unspeakable deed. The house is just overgrown with weeds.'

'What has she done?'

'It's too horrible for words.' Said his wife and just stared innocently at her husband.

1 In ancient times only nobles were allowed to wear their hair in a topknot.

Chapter Nine
GRANNY TAEJU

For tens of years Granny Taeju had lived in the old tile-roofed house which was encircled by a stone wall and which was variously called The House of the Shrine, The House of the Spirits, The House without Gables, or simply The Haunted House.

At first there had lived a Taoist master of unknown past. When the master left this old woman, who had until then looked after the village laundry had this house all to herself. Six months later she started telling fortunes, claiming that the Taoist master had passed on to her his knowledge of Taoist magic. But whether it was because her magic was feeble her predictions had the reputation of being unreliable. Soon afterwards she claimed suddenly that she had been possessed by the spirit of a baby girl who had died of smallpox, and from doing Taoist fortune-telling she became Granny Taeju, who did 'Myongdo' (spirit) fortune-telling. At the same time her fortune-telling became marvellously accurate so that her fame spread far and near, so that four or five months later the fame of the 'Fortune-teller of the Haunted House outside the City Walls', spread not only to the immediate neighbourhood but all over the district. At about this time Granny Taeju suddenly disappeared.

Six months before this a child had disappeared from Hwangnam-ri. The four-year-old boy had been playing in the road in front of his house when he disappeared. At that time a tug of war was held on the street that ran from the village of Bongwhangdae to the village of Hwangnam-ri, so that the place was seething with people all over the place. Parents and kin, each was allocated an area in which to look for the boy and they entered each house and searched every nook and cranny, but of the boy there was not a trace.

Three or four months passed like this and the parents had almost abandoned all hope of finding the child. Since the child's family and the Chung's who lived outside the city walls were related by marriage, Lady Chung asked Eulhwa who had come to prepare a rite. Eulhwa answered:

'It is better to consult a spirit fortune-teller rather than a shaman.'

'Of course, so we went and asked the spirit fortune-teller who told us that the tiger of Mt. Sundo had carried the boy off.'

Eulhwa for some reason shook her head from side to side.

'Why do you shake your head like that?'

'The tiger of Mt. Sundo does not come down during the big tug-of-war,' insisted Eulhwa as if she and the tiger were neighbours.

But Lady Chung did not question her any more about this. Rather, as if it was something certain she asked:

'Then Granny Myung-do must have been lying, isn't it?'

Eulhwa did not answer and just asked:

'How old is the granny's familiar spirit?'

'Granny's familiar spirit' meant the age of the child who had died and become a 'Myongdo' or familiar spirit. In other words this question asked the age of the child who had died and had become the familiar spirit of the Granny Myongdo.

'They say he is four or five, I think.'

'How old is the child they are looking for?'

'Kiho is also four years old.'

'Oh, what was the voice like?'

'Voice?'

'Did the voices resemble each other?'

'Whose voices?'

'I mean the voice of the familiar spirit and the voice of Kiho.'

'I don't know. Why do you ask?'

To tell the truth, Lady Chung had never paid much

attention to Granny Taeju's spirit-possessed voice, and did not have the slightest memory of Kiho's voice. Hence she could not tell whether the two voices resembled each other or not. What did bother her was rather why Eulhwa was so inquisitive about this matter.

Eulhwa again did not bother to answer and said:

'The boy's mother must know if she listens carefully.'

'She went with me the last time and she did not say that the voice particularly resembled that of her child.'

As if discomforted Eulhwa just looked at Lady Chung then lowered her eyes.

'Do you think that the child ghost that possesses the old Granny is that of Kiho?'

Eulhwa did not answer, but her expression seemed to indicate that this might be true.

'I don't think that is true. Because, we still don't know whether the child is dead or alive. Besides if he is dead, don't they say that fortune-telling ghosts are just the ghosts of children dead of smallpox or measles?'

Eulhwa opened her mouth as if to say something and then she closed it again. It seemed that she could see something but was reluctant to say it out aloud.

Three days later, when Kiho's mother came from Hwangnam-ri to see her and Lady Chung related this conversation to her, Kiho's mother said immediately:

'That may be true,' and she added, 'Our Kiho is probably dead.'

'He may be dead, but they say that only ghosts of children dead from smallpox or measles may become fortune-telling ghosts.'

'They say that need not be so. Any child that age can become one if he dies before his time . . .'

'If you absolutely think so, let us go and see this Myongdo Granny once more . . .'

And with these words the two women went to look for the Granny Taeju of the House without Gables. That day, when at first she saw Lady Chung, Granny Taeju looked over-joyed to see her, but when she saw Kiho's mother following Lady Chung she asked with a scared expression on her face.

'Who is that?'

'Don't you know, this is the Lady from Hwangnam-ri who lost her child.'

'Didn't I say the last time that the tiger of Mt. Sundo must have carried it off?'

Granny Taeju broke in unpleasantly with a dissatisfied expression on her face. Seeing that the woman from Hwangnam-ri was too shy to say anything, Lady Chung said:

'No, that's not why she came to see you today. Since last coming here she has lost a silver ring. She tells me that she would like to find out where it has gone, as well as talk about a rite for her baby carried off by the tiger.'

In this way did she concoct up some excuse on the spot.

Since she was indebted to Lady Chung in many ways, and since she thought of her as her patron, she said without further hesitation.

'Is that so? Well then, please sit down. When and where did you lose your silver ring?'

And she made preparations to call up the spirit of the dead child that possessed her. Granny Taeju kowtowed twice toward the altar and pulled out the table on which various divining instruments were laid, and which had been covered by a cloth. On the dish on top of the table there was a rattle. She picked up the rattle and shook it a couple of times, replaced it on the dish, then closed her eyes, and head bowed and facing the table, silently recited some words of an incantation. Rapt with attention, Kiho's mother listened with bated breath, but all she could hear were the words 'Hwangnam-ri', 'Mrs. Lee', 'silver ring', which could be heard intermittently.

Having finished her incantation the old woman made a whistling sound. Then the corner of the black handkerchief flapped slightly as if disturbed by a faint gust of wind, and there was a faint and almost inaudible twittering, like the sound of a small bird in some far-distant forest. Granny Taeju lifted her head and looked at the flapping black handkerchief. Then it seemed that amongst the twittering were the words 'single chest', 'butterfly casket'. Suddenly, the woman from Hwangnam-ri, who had been listening with rapt attention, exclaimed: 'Oh! Kiho.' and screamed to burst her throat and collapsed on the floor.

The barely audible sound, like the faint twittering of some small and diseased bird in a far-distant forest, stopped abruptly, together with the faint flapping of the black handkerchief.

Full of fury, Granny Taeju glared with eyes glittering viciously at the woman from Hwangnam-ri who lay prostrate on the floor.

'Mother of Kiho, Mother of Kiho.'

Lady Chung shook the Hwangnam-ri woman's shoulder. The woman remained unconscious.

'Hurry outside and fetch me a bowl of cold water.'

Lady Chung ordered the old woman, as if she was telling her off. In a voice full of fury Granny Taeju spat viciously:

'That woman has been struck by a curse.'

Lady Chung roared back.

'Since she has been struck down in your house can you not even produce a bowl of water? Since she has been curse-stricken whilst attending your familiar spirit, who else can be blamed but the witch to whom the familiar spirit belongs.'

Granny Taeju put the table beneath the altar and got up, staring at the fallen woman.

'Please regain your senses, Mother of Kiho.' Lady Chung again shook the woman's shoulder, whose eyes were still closed, but now she seemed to be breathing. Granny Taeju pushed in a bowl of cold water into the room and spat the water she had in her mouth at the face of the unconscious woman. Her eyes started to flutter open.

'Mother of Kiho, Mother of Kiho, come to your senses.'

'Oh . . . L. .a. .d. .y'

Barely able to speak the woman called out thus in a low voice.

Her face still red and swollen with rage, Granny Taeju stared at the woman with eyes filled with hatred. She shut the door and went out. Lady Chung and the woman were left alone in the room. Though they waited the owner of the room, Granny Taeju, did not come back in. It was a mystery as to where she had gone and what she was doing.

'Strange, where has this woman gone that she does not come back?'

Lady Chung mumbled to herself and looked in the direction of the woman from Hwangnam-ri and asked.

'How are you, Mother of Kiho? Can you get up and walk now?'

'Lady, I don't think I can go back.'

'Why? Have you not yet regained your senses?'

'No, Lady, my Kiho is in this room. How can I leave when my Kiho is in this room?'

'Look here, don't all familiar spirits behave like that? They just twitter and they all sound alike. Since all familiar spirits that tell fortunes were all children of more or less the same age, is it not natural that they all sound alike?'

'No, Lady, it is my Kiho, without a shred of doubt. I heard my Kiho's voice.'

'Then why didn't you know when you came here before? If you say it is Kiho, then it must have been Kiho's voice on that occasion as well.'

'At that time the witch did not call her familiar but just muttered any old gibberish. At that time even the black handkerchief on the wall was absent.'

On hearing the Hwangnam-ri woman's words it seemed to Lady Chung that on occasion the old witch did not call up her familiar but had just made up some gibberish about the tiger of Mt. Sundo.

'How dare that old witch do such a thing pretending to call up her familiar and muttering any old rubbish that suited her, when she knows what a huge debt she owes me. Let this old hag just show her face here, and let's see if I can't drag a confession out of her.' So thought Lady Chung, eagerly awaiting the old woman. But the Granny Taeju did not come.

The two women waited. When black dusk shrouded dark pictures that covered the four walls, they came out of the room. It was already dark, and the woman from Hwangnam-ri could not walk, her body still shaking from the shock of encountering the familiar. It was decided that she should sleep at Lady Chung's that night and then set off to see Granny Taeju the following morning.

After supper Lady Chung said:

'Now that I think, the witch was possessed by a familiar spirit about a week after Kiho's disappearance. So it may be that Kiho's ghost had become a divining ghost and latched itself on to the old witch as her familiar.'

The woman from Hwangnam-ri answered:

'There is not a slightest trace of doubt. No one but my Kiho would know such a thing.'

'Why need that be so? A divining spirit is a ghost of a dead child, so although it may not have any opinions of its own it should be as sharp as nails at looking for lost things and telling where they are . . .'

'No, Lady, it is not that.'

'Not that? . . .'

'The chattering of divining spirits when they have found something may be alike, but this one said something that only my Kiho could have said.'

'What is that?'

'Did it not say that the silver ring was in the butterfly casket in the single chest of drawers? If it was any other child who had died and become a ghost it would have said that the ring was in the trinket box in the yellow cabinet.'

As she said this she stared at Lady Chung's face. As it seemed that Lady Chung still did not fully understand, she added.

'It is only in our family that a "yellow cabinet" is called the "single chest" and a "trinket box" a "butterfly casket". So only members of my family know these words. I have heard the divining ghost of a dead child before, and the ghost could only speak words that it had used as a living child.'

Then Lady Chung nodded as if she had more or less understood and asked:

'Well, is it true that the silver ring is in the . . . what did you say it was called? . . . the single chest . . . the butterfly box?'

Lady Chung wanted to know this since Granny Taeju had refused to divine the whereabouts of the child, saying that she had already done this once before, and hence had spouted out any old gibberish as if it had been an incantation.

'Of course, it is there just as it was when I first came to the new house as bride.'

'Then it seems that when Kiho died his ghost fastened itself onto the old witch.'

The woman from Hwangnam-ri said nothing and just turned her face to one side.

'What is it?'

'I heard my Kiho calling me then. I am sure I heard him call out Mummy, Mummy! And I swear his voice when he cried out for me was so piteous that I fainted on the spot.'

'You say his voice seemed so piteous?'

'I cannot find words to frame it. It made my flesh creep, and the heart in my bosom shrank back and shrivelled up on itself.'

'Well, since he disappeared like that he must have met with a wretched end. Is that not why he became a witch's familiar that cries out other people's fortune?'

The woman from Hwangnam-ri said nothing. A long while later she asked.

'But why did that Granny Myongdo run away like that?'

'Well, are spirit-possessed witches like ordinary mortals? Do they not act like madmen to begin with?'

And the two women stopped their talk at that.

The next day the woman from Hwangnam-ri had a scanty breakfast and went to see Granny Taeju. But the Granny still had not come back. It was a house too fearful in which to await alone so she ran off to the Chung's to tell the lady.

'How odd!' said Lady Chung, and put on the formal skirt that she wore for outings and raced off with the woman to the House without Gables. The house was still empty. Lady Chung opened the door and went in the room and looked about. She said:

'Why, this witch has run away!'

'Run away?' exclaimed the woman in surprise.

'Seeing that the silk wrapping cloth had disappeared from the cabinet it seems that she just packed her valuables and ran off. She can't have done such a thing! And still owing me fifty ryang! . . .'

'Oh, Lady, I think I shall die if I don't meet that woman.'

So saying, the woman from Hwangnam-ri collapsed in a heap on the floor sobbing out aloud.

'Though I have to go to China to get her I shall catch this old bitch so do not be worried and please get up.'

And she led the woman up by her sleeve.

Lady Chung sent people out everywhere to look for Granny Taeju, but no one knew where she was. And the woman from Hwangnam-ri, who could not just sit and wait until the Lady found the Granny Taeju, also went searching any place that was said to house a sorceress or a diviner.

She had heard of Eulhwa the Sorceress of Jatshil from Lady Chung, so she dropped in on the way from Angang in order to ask her in person about this matter.

Having heard the tale from the woman Eulhwa nodded and
said:

'That sounds likely, that sounds likely.'

The woman asked:

'Why did you think so from the beginning?'

'When I was told that the tiger of Mt. Sundo had carried
him off I knew at once that it was a lie. The tiger of Mt. Sundo
never comes down for the big tug of war. If that is the case,
why would that old woman lie? I thought "That old woman
and the lost child must have some connexion." So I told Lady
Chung that you would know if you listened well to the old
woman's familiar.'

'Oh, why didn't I come and see you in the beginning? I
should have retold the story in more detail to Lady Chung.'

'I knew at once when I heard this story about the tiger. I felt
suspicious of the old woman. But it seemed that Lady Chung
trusted the old woman and I had no proof, so I did not explain
things fully.'

'Well, what do you think? Tell me what you know. I will
pay you back for the services you have rendered me. When I
think I heard Kiho's voice in that old woman's room even now
I feel like going mad. How did Kiho attach himself to that old
woman?'

Tears were glistening in the woman's eyes. Even as she said
this the woman from Hwangnam-ri knew of the belief that a
child dead of smallpox or measles would become a divining
ghost, but when she thought on how Kiho's ghost could have
latched itself onto that old woman of all people, her head spun
round and round.

'Have you not heard that if a woman wishes to be possessed
by a divining ghost, she cuts off the tip of the little finger of
the dead child and carries it on her person or puts it in her
house, so that the ghost of the child will latch itself onto her as
a divining ghost?'

'Well, yes, I have heard such a thing, but our Kiho was alive
and well, and he didn't even know the old woman.'

'That is why it is so horrible,' said Eulhwa in a low voice as
if to herself.

Not understanding Eulhwa, the woman from Hwangnam-ri
looked at her for a long time.

'Please save me. That old woman must come back home in

secret but I am too scared to wait for her alone. Please keep me company just for one night, when I wait for the old woman in that room.' She begged her grabbing her wrist.

'Well, let us go then.'

And Eulhwa followed the woman out.

The two women first dropped by Lady Chung's and had supper together and together with Lady Chung the three of them went to the witch house. Lighting an oil wick in the old woman's room three women talked far into the night. When Lady Chung left, the two remaining women lay down wordlessly in wait for something. They had the vague expectation that the old woman would drop in stealthily during the night.

Though they waited past midnight there was no sign of anyone. Then, the woman from Hwangnam-ri, who had been wandering about all day without a bite to eat began to breathe raggedly and soon dropped off to sleep. Listening to the thin breathing of the woman, Eulhwa's eyelids also started to close. It was then. From somewhere a sound like a child crying could be heard snivelling. Eulhwa at once thought of Yongsul when she had sent him to the temple. Well it could not be Yongsul.

'Who are you?' asked Eulhwa.

The crying stopped and at the same time her eyes closed again. Whether in sleep or awake she faintly heard again that snivelling crying.

'Who are you?' asked Eulhwa again.

The sobbing crying turned into a sound like a sleeping baby breathing raggedly in its blankets.

'Who are you?' she asked for the third time.

The ragged breathing sounded like 'mummy, mummy.' Yes, you must be Kiho. Are you Kiho? 'Mummy, mummy, take me home' answered the ragged breathing. Where are you? Mummy I am here, behind the kitchen, by the wall . . .

The snivelling and the breathing stopped.

. . . Eulhwa opened her eyes, but she could not tell whether she had heard that snivelling crying in a dream or lying awake with just her eyes closed.

Early that morning Eulhwa and the Hwangnam-ri woman opened the kitchen door and went out into the back garden. The back garden was overgrown with weeds except for one spot which was covered with dry grass. They pulled away the dry grass and dug away some earth with a trowel. A piece of red cloth and a lock of child's hair was revealed.

'Ah, Kiho!'

The Hwangnam-ri woman screamed and fainted on the spot.

It was about a fortnight later. There was a rumour that a woman resembling the former Granny Taeju had been seen at Punhwang Temple. At once the Hwangnam-ri woman rushed off to Punhwang Temple. According to one priest a nun with unshaved head who fitted the description had been seen there from about a month before. The Hwangnam-ri woman wandered for three days about the temple and finally caught the old woman, dressed in a nun's garb in front of the temple gate. But upon catching the old woman the Hwangnam-ri woman could only say:

'What have you done with my Kiho?' and promptly fainted on the spot.

When the old woman tried to brush off the Hwangnam-ri woman and run away, a farmer who happened to be passing caught the old woman.

'What is up?'

'It is some woman who has nothing to do with me.'

'If she has nothing to do with you why did she grab hold of you and fall down?'

While they tussled a crowd gathered about them, and in the end the Hwangnam-ri woman and the old witch were taken to Lady Chung.

The Hwangnam-ri woman, who had regained consciousness said:

'Lady, if I let this old hag go before I see her break, I shall die.'

'Don't worry, of course we shall see her break.'

Lady Chung put the old woman in an empty storeroom. Every day she opened the storeroom and asked:

'Will you still not give up?'

'Please, Lady, at least save my life.'

Their conversation always ended like this. Lady Chung did not give the old woman a bite to eat. Three days passed. The old woman was utterly exhausted.

'Will you still not give up?'

'Please Lady, at least let me live.'

'If you confess I will let you live. Will you still not give up?'

The old woman was silent.

'If I let you go like this you will be torn to death by Kiho's family. If you confess at once I shall at least save your vile life.'

'Lady!'

'Hurry up and confess.'

'I deserve to die.'

'Talk!'

'I took the baby.'

'And?'

'I killed him by confining him in a pot.'

'Oh, you evil creature!'

Lady Chung could not contain her rage. She seized the old witch by the hair and dashed her to the ground. The old woman lay as one dead.

'Talk if you want to go out of here alive.' At these words the old woman sat up. But she was not able to continue talking.

'Will you not talk?'

At these words the old woman again raised her head.

'Well did a child as old as four go into the pot without resisting?'

'First I tied his limbs and fastened a cloth about his mouth so that he could not speak, and I lay him down in a corner of the room. When all the strength was gone out of him I put him in the pot.'

'Oh, you monster!' And the Lady ground her teeth.

As if she thought that it made no difference since she had confessed so far, the old woman poured out the rest of the story.

The child remained alive in the pot for four days. The old woman first gave the child in the pot a cup of red water. As the child had been starving he drank it without even distinguishing what it was. The second day, she gave a cup of blue water. The child also drank that up. The third day she gave a cup of yellow water. On the fourth day she gave a cup of black water. The child dropped the cup from his fingers without having finished even half of it. When the woman opened the lid of the pot the child was dead.

The old woman recited the incantation:

'Child, child, follow me,' and cut off the tip of the child's little finger with a pair of scissors. She wrapped it in black silk and carried it on her person attached to her underwear. She buried the corpse in the back yard.

When she had finished hearing the story Lady Chung was so horrified that her body shook all over. Of such matters as why the old woman had to feed red, blue, yellow and black water to the child, and why she had to cut off the little finger, she did not even think of asking.

'You shall be punished by heaven for your crime. I should drag you off now to the authorities, but since I have known you for long, and since I have promised to save your life, I cannot do that. Leave here at once. Not for a moment do I want to have a monster like you in my house. Leave for some far-off place at once. As you owe me money and even though no one will live in that ghost house of yours, I shall take it as my own. Do not even think of showing your face here again.'

When the Lady finished her command the old woman who had been lying down got up and sat up.

'Did you say ghost house? That is so. No one but ghosts shall be able to live there.' And with these words she vanished tottering into the dark.

Chapter Ten
RITE AND MASS

When Park Kunshik heard the story of Granny Taeju from his wife, he breathed a long sigh and said:

'Why did I not become a monk?' He then ordered wine to be brought in.

Although he did not usually like to drink, that night he drank alone long into the night. He fell asleep dead drunk and did not get up for five days.

A week later he barely managed to change into his formal clothes and went to see Scholar Choi. He told him of what he had heard from his wife and said:

'When I realized that our enemies were not only the Japs, I felt so dizzy that I took to bed.'

He then declared his intention to give up everything and go into the mountains.

'What? You become a monk?' asked Choi Kam in a disgruntled tone.

'Yes, sir. I have lost the desire to do anything. People kill one another for myriad reasons, but to seduce such a young thing and to kill it in such a way! When I think that I am of one blood with such wicked and vicious people, I find it fearful and repulsive to look upon people's faces and I think only of going to hide in a desert island or in the deepest mountain.'

'Do you think that I don't know your thoughts? If you too forsake this world, only such vicious and wicked people will be left. In such a situation should it not be the case that such people should remain in the world to enlighten it. Such a deed is due to ignorance and foolishness. So you must enlighten people so that no such people remain. When you came back from Seoul saying that the resistance movement must start with an enlightenment of the people, was I not all for it, saying that I would help all I could. So do not talk like a weakling and let your resolve be as firm as steel.'

Park Kunshik said nothing.

'If you become a monk, will such people disappear? If you become a monk and enter a temple, you will meet that old woman there. The reason is because for such old women the temple is also their last place of refuge. To begin with, did not that Granny Taeju also flee to a temple when her sins were discovered? Did they not say she was caught at Punhwang Temple? It is like that. Please do not think of becoming a monk. However angry you may be, please remain in this world. If you really cannot bear things, come to me and share a cup of wine.'

Park Kunshik could not bear to reject Choi Kam's urgent plea. After a month later Park Kunshik came back from his cousin's sixtieth birthday ceremony at Taegu and went to see Choi Kam, saying:

'I heard of Christianity on the way back from celebrating my paternal cousin's sixtieth birthday at Taegu. As people say that Christianity is the fastest way of banishing superstition, I am thinking of adopting Christianity, sir.'

Again with sour face, Choi Kam said:

'Are you and I not originally Confucianists? This is the way of our ancestors, and it is also the Primal Way. So it is not a good idea to convert to Buddhism or Christianity. But if your purpose is to banish superstition I think Christianity is better than Buddhism. The reason being, I have heard that Buddhism does not reject heathen idols whereas Christianity does so absolutely.'

'I am grateful to you, sir, for giving me such leeway. I would like to become a Christian and banish superstition.'

So saying, Park Kunshik left Choi Kam's. This also became a farewell to Choi Kam. For Choi Kam was most upset at Park's conversion.

When Yongsul heard of the story of Granny Taeju from Park Kunshik it was as if he had heard both the life story of

Park Kunshik and the history of the house in which his mother Eulhwa lived. From that time on Yongsul went to see him every day. Early in the morning he left his house and went to see Park, asking if there was anything which needed his help. He then went to pray at the church. He did more or less that same thing when he came back from church. So consequently he spent much time under Park's care acting as deacon.

Although Park Kunshik did not give Yongsul any wise thoughts or clever plans on how to dispose his mother of her superstitious beliefs, the very fact that he was there was a great relief to Yongsul. To begin with it gave him the peace of mind to look out for any opportunity to lead his mother to the correct path.

To Yongsul, another encouraging fact was the fact that his step sister had begun to regain her powers of speech. To him, who believed that Wolhie had been struck dumb as a result of being possessed of an evil spirit, and the fact that she was slowly regaining her powers of speech was a sure sign that the spirit was releasing its hold on her. Of course he interpreted this as a result of God being moved by his daily prayer. Hence he felt that there was no reason why Wolhie should not understand God's love.

Youngsul went home, thinking that now was the time to teach Wolhie and make her repent of her past. When she saw him come in, Wolhie had been painting, put her brush down and greeted her brother with glad face:

'Elder brother!'

'Wolhie, can you hear me?'

Silently Wolhie smiled and nodded. Yongsul also smiled warmly and said:

'God loves you, and has driven away the evil ghost inside you.'

With a face full of surprise Wolhie said:

'God?'

It seemed that that was the only word she had understood.

'God who resides in heaven.' And Yongsul pointed up to heaven, speaking slowly, but she did not seem to understand at all and just stared at him with stupid face. Yongsul took out a bible from his bosom.

'What God hath shown and taught us is contained in this book.' So saying he held the bible open and began to read:

'Matthew Chapter 9 verse 32: As they went out, behold, they brought to him a dumb man possessed with a devil. And when the devil was cast out, the dumb spake: and the multitudes marvelled, saying: It was never so in Israel. But the Pharisees said, He casteth out devils through the prince of devils.'

Yongsul read thus far and lifted his head to look at Wolhie's face. She was looking at a fly crawling along the floor. Seeing that she did not understand very well he explained to her with a regretful face.

'Listen well, Dalhie, Jesus has cured one, who like you was possessed by a spirit and made dumb. In a word that is your story. Be off foul ghost, said Jesus and the ghost fled and like you the man was able to speak. You know, don't you?'

Wolhie was silent. With a worried look on her face she shook her head back and forth. For some reason Yongsul sniggered and said:

'You will soon know,' and opened his bible again.

'Listen Dalhie, this is written in Matthew Chapter 12. This is also about one struck dumb by an evil spirit . . . Then was brought unto him one possessed with a devil, blind and dumb: and he healed him, insomuch that the blind and dumb both spake and saw. And all the people were amazed and said, Is not this the son of David? . . .'

With great enthusiasm Yongsul read on, but Wolhie just looked at him with stupid eyes. Yongsul took his eyes off the bible and looking at her asked:

'How is that?' His face was full of pride.

Not understanding a thing Wolhie just shook her head from side to side. Bending Yongsul pointed to the pictures of various shaman deities pasted on the four walls and said:

'Mother has pasted pictures of ghosts all over the house so that you too have become possessed by one and have lost your power of speech. But long ago Jesus had chased away all such ghosts so that the people were cured of their illnesses and regained the power of speech. I too have prayed to Jesus to drive out the ghost that possesses you, so you must believe in Jesus together with me. Then you shall no longer be tormented by ghosts and you shall be able to speak properly and get to know God.'

Full of fervour and belief he explained things to her, but

Wolhie just looked at him with eyes that were dreaming of some far-distant dream land.

'Jesus?' she asked.

She did not even know what the word 'Jesus' meant. She had heard the word 'God' a few times from her mother, but she had never before heard the word 'Jesus'. Nor did she know why Yongsul kept on using the words 'Jesus' and 'God'.

'That is so. You must believe in Jesus. Since God resides in heaven, Jesus came in lieu of him to the world.'

When Yongsul was saying this there came from outside the words:

'Daughter, daughter, my daughter!'

Yongsul quickly hid his bible in his breast and opened the door of the room. Eulhwa was roaring drunk.

'Daughter, daughter, my daughter!

Sul, Sul, my son!'

On seeing her children Eulhwa started to sing, swaying side to side in a dance. Yongsul was dead ashamed of his mother but did not show it and entered the room ahead of her. Eulhwa who had followed him in called him in a kind of voice as if she bore glad tidings.

'Sul,' she continued. 'You've talked to our Dalhie, haven't you? What do you think? Don't you think she speaks much better than before?'

'I think so too, mother.'

'That is so. All that is thanks to you. It seems that our Dalhie has been invigorated and is happy since you have come. She seems to love you very much. She will soon be able to talk properly.'

Thus did Eulhwa try to flatter Yongsul, who watched her carefully to find out what her ulterior motive was. Eulhwa continued:

'Well, that is inevitable. Since I am always out, doesn't that young thing keep house all by herself? If it was any other girl they would have run away, do you think that they would have stayed? With things as they are, all of a sudden in pops her brother so you can imagine how happy she is. Her eyes shine, her ears shall become sharp, her mind becomes clear and her mouth opens all by itself.'

Even when she was talking with her family when words grew

long she would break out unconsciously into the narrative chant that she used for rites. Not only was he ashamed of his mother when she was like this, but without his knowing his heart secretly rebelled. Even now, as his mother said: 'Eyes shall shine and ears shall become sharp,' he could not bear to listen but closed his eyes in prayer.

'Sul!'

Surprised by his mother's voice he opened his eyes. With eyes full of fear that his mother would read his thoughts as always, he looked at her.

Smiling gently she said:

'When we have the big rite, go with Dalhie to the temple. I may be able to go as well.'

As if she had understood her mother's words Wolhie looked at Yongsul with eyes that never before had shone so brilliantly. It struck Yongsul that he must act now and refuse her offer. He muttered:

'Mother, I . . .' He then gathered courage and said: 'I don't want to go to the temple.'

He used the native dialect in order not to offend his mother.

'Why's that? Don't you want to cure your half-deaf sister?'

'No, it is the priests at the temple that I don't wish to see.'

Youngsul was afraid that if he told the truth and said that he could not go because he was a Christian, this would anger his mother so he made up this excuse.

'Sul!'

At Eulhwa's gentle voice he finally was put at ease. He looked at her in the face.

'My son, who art as fair as the moon, we could really have an enjoyable time were it not for your Jesus or Jasus. Look at your sister. Isn't she beautiful? Would an angel from heaven be fairer, would she be clearer if she were carved out of jade? If only she could speak, then there would be no couple in the world that could match you for looks or for beauty.'

'Please don't worry mother, Dalhie will soon be able to speak.'

'Yes, well, since your arrival here her speech has been slowly coming back to her. I shall entrust her to you so do your best.'

Why did Eulhwa say this? That she entrusts Wolhie to her son with whom she had been so dissatisfied and careful. Did this mean that if only he were able to cure Wolhie's dumbness, his mother would not mind Wolhie believing in God? Thinking that this was his chance he said:

'Mother, if you entrust Dalhie to me I shall take full responsibility and cure her.'

Eulhwa seemed to be thinking for an instance, then asked:

'Where will you take her?'

Thinking that this was a problem that had to be faced, sooner or later, Yongsul answered:

'I shall take her to church.'

'What is church? Is it where you do Jesus?'

'Yes, mother. I have been praying every day at the church. I have been praying to God that our Wolhie's tongue become free and that her ears become sharp, and that she can speak without hindrance . . .'

As he said this he watched his mother's reaction. Since his mother acknowledged that Wolhie's speech had much improved, if she knew that this was thanks to his prayer, her bias against Christianity would also be loosened, thought Yongsul. But without giving him even time to think, Eulhwa denied this.

'No,' and she continued. 'It is not because you offered sacrifice to the church. Our Dalhie has always lived alone in a corner of the room and you are the first person she has met. If you had not done this Jesus but had taken her instead to the temple her speech would have improved much more than it has.'

Eulhwa said this as if to mock her son's foolishness. In his heart Yongsul wished to retort that the reason why Wolhie lost her speech was not because she had been cooped up all alone in the corner of the room, but that it had arisen when he and her father were all together with her under one roof. But he did not want to upset his mother so he professed gently.

'Mother, that happened a long time ago when I still lived with Wolhie and you.'

'Yes, there you are right.'

Eulhwa meekly acknowledged this but she continued to assert that her opinion was right.

'But things are different now. She will get better even if she just has someone to play with.'

'Well then, why don't you take her with you when you go out?'

97

At Yongsul's words, Eulhwa said nothing for a long while, then asked in a low voice:

'She cannot go together with me to the taverns, can she?'

'If it were at the rites I could take her with me, but I couldn't take care of her during the rites, and besides, what will happen if someone steals her? There are no two Dalhies in the world, you know.'

It seemed that she was asking him to come with Wolhie to the rites.

'Mother, what do you think about this? We shall take her once to the rites and once to the church and ask her which one she prefers . . . .'

'Attend rites, attend Jesus and ask which she likes better, did you say?'

Sensing a challenge in her son's words she asked him thus. Yongsul did not wish to place the rites on an equal standing with the church so he kept silent. Eulhwa mistook this for a retreat on her son's part due to lack of confidence and asked:

'Why don't you answer? You are afraid now that we can compare, aren't you?'

'No, mother.'

'No? Fine. Let's do as you say. On 21st of this month I perform the great rite at Master Chung's. Let you bring Dalhie there. And after that take her to your Jesus business. Do you understand?'

Yongsul was silent.

'Why don't you answer? Are you shivering with fear?'

'No.'

'Then?'

'Let me think on it for one more night.'

'Think on it for one more night? Yes, do as you like. But it is not a manly thing for you to vacillate like that. If it is something you will do, do it at once, and if you cannot do it, say so at once, but do not waver undecided saying I shall leave this decision for tomorrow or the day after. If you believe like that you shall never be able to do great things.'

Yongsul did not answer. He had decided to ignore whatever his mother said, and delay all decisions until further council with Elder Park.

The next day, when he had heard Yongsul, Park Kunshik asked:

'Are you convinced that your sister's dumbness is caused by one of those devils such as those which come out in the Bible?'

'I am certain, sir. When she was young she could speak with no hindrance, so we cannot say that her throat or tongue is deformed. Moreover since she started to grow up she has been oppressed by shaman ghosts. When I returned and started to pray for her clearly her speech came back to her, so without any doubt she is one of those struck dumb by a devil that has possessed her.'

'Then do you believe that taking her to church will restore her speech?'

'Yes.'

'Then go ahead. Is it not true that you have never thought of the rite as something that equals the church? So if you go and attend rites and not by your own volition, would this not be just to cure your sister and not out of any other reason?'

'Yes, that is so. My first purpose is to cure my sister, but things do not stop there.'

'What other purpose do you have?' asked Park, worried.

'As I told you sir, my original purpose is to dispossess my mother and sister of shaman ghosts and make them believe in Jesus. To accomplish this, if I first take my sister to church and cast out her ghost and give her back the power of speech, then this shall also be a good occasion to convert my mother.'

'That is even better. You need not falter any more.'

Park Kunshik looked gratified.

Chapter Eleven
THE PRINCESS OF THE DEAD

The Great Rite for the Late Master Chung took place in the garden of the Chung's. It took place because many fortune-tellers had all claimed that the spirit of Master Chung Mansu, who had died three years ago was wandering about this house unable to cross over to the otherworld. This was a certainty, according to the fortune-tellers, since after his death his family often fell sick and especially because of the symptoms of Byunghyun, his younger grandson. Byunghyun was twelve that year and due to some unknown ailment he limped or went blind or ran a high fever and no medicine seemed to cure his illness.

When Eulhwa performed a rite the symptoms went away, only to come back soon afterwards. So Lady Chung had asked Eulhwa from the very beginning if the old man's spirit had suffered some mishap, but always Eulhwa did not give a satisfactory answer saying:

'Perhaps that may be true but . . .''

Lady Chung went to consult with other fortune-tellers and spirit-diviners who all agreed in saying that the place was haunted by the spirit of the old man. When she told this to Eulhwa, Eulhwa just said:

'I also thought that but . . .'

Neither did Lady Chung say any more of the matter. Eulhwa had always made it clear that she was not a fortune-telling shaman, and never proposed any rite whether big or small to anyone. Since Eulhwa was this family's regular shaman and hence responsible for performing the House Spirit rite and the Big Dipper rite taking place on the first and the fifteenth of each month, it went without saying that she should perform the great rite which would send the dead spirit to the otherworld. Since everyone acknowledged that Eulhwa never undertook an exorcism for the sake of earning money, and since the Hwangnam woman asked her, as if to tell her off, why she had not told Lady Chung, who was her regular client, of the matter.

'I was afraid that it would bring down the wrath of my host goddess on myself.' This meant that if she undertook something she had never done before she might bring down the wrath of her host goddess the Lady Sunwang of Mt. Sundo.

Eulhwa's Great Rite was already something which made the whole village shake with excitement, and added to that the host was the famous Master and on top of everything Lady Chung was renowned as a life long patron of the rites, so this rite was really something not to be missed.

That night people started gathering from the early evening and packed the spacious garden. Later on even the alley next to the study was packed and when toffee-vendors, cake-sellers, vendors of drink and other foodstuff started crowding in it became hard to push one's way through the crowd.

In his heart Yongsul thought it a rare stroke of luck that there was no moon and there was such a crowd, since no one then was able to see his face.

But since Wolhie was a little deaf, and since he had promised his mother, he was obliged to take her up to the offering table. From the awning above the table were hanging lanterns covered in a rainbow tapestry of many coloured threads, and he had to keep his head bowed to avoid banging against them.

But apart from his promise to his mother, Yongsul was also interested in watching Wolhie's face to see what reaction she showed, so he could not just jump up and run away. If there was another reason, it was that if he could get a close look at the rites and the shaman and this whole world of superstition it would help him to fight these superstitions.

But Wolhie was free of such a critical and negative attitude.

She was looking at the magnificently arrayed food on the table and the dazzling rainbow-coloured lampshade with eyes goggled with wonder and curiosity. When Eulhwa shook the rattle to summon the dead person her shoulders even started to move up and down in time to the music.

In the beginning, Eulhwa occasionally would cast a glance towards Wolhie and Yongsul, but when she started shaking the rattle she seemed to forget their very existence. She started singing in her sad and inimitable way:

'Come back, come back
Come back, dead one
To the birthcord of your father
To the milkline of your mother
Be it ten years
Be it hundred
Come back to this palace.
Will you come if rice cooked
In a bronze cauldron buds?
Will you come if the rice under
The cupboard sprouts?
Can you not come
Because your clothes are
Soaked by June showers?
Can you not come
Because you have fallen ill
After visiting someone sick?
If you come back
In the spring time
Flowers shall bloom
Leaves shall form.
Our life, wandering about
This floating world
Once we are gone
We cannot come back.
Is this not sad, Oh, dead one
Hurry, hurry and come back.

Eulhwa's hoarse and lamenting voice seemed to swallow up the hue and cry of the bursting crowd. Her slender waist undulated and whenever her slender arms rose up and down the three male shamans played their drums and cymbals and tartar fiddles in rhythm. Even the crowd seemed to breathe in and breathe out automatically in rhythm to this.

When Eulhwa had stopped singing the song that summoned the dead one, a woman who had been sitting next to Yongsul half arose then sat down again. She pointed to the offering table and said:

'Look! Lady Chung has changed into new clothes and is sitting out there to greet her dead Lord.'

'Well, well, it seems they shall greet each other for the last time.'

'Why doesn't the old man fly off to the underworld instead of remaining here?'

'Well, with so much land and so many precious sons and daughters not to mention grandchildren, wouldn't you be thinking of this world?'

It was the two women talking again. Then the woman facing them said to the old woman next to her:

'What do you mean, Granny? If everyone became a wandering ghost because of regrets in this world who would there be left to go straight to the otherworld?'

'Well, isn't that why shamans and their male assistants make a living.'

Then an old man spoke behind Yongsul to someone.

'Since the late Master Chung's wife worships ghosts so much he must have come back to receive one last offering. If he receives the Great Rite from Eulhwa the gates of the afterworld will be flung open for him and he can leave satisfied with a light heart.'

Listening to the shaman's words and the mumbling of the spectators, Yongsul was struck by a curious thought. He started to have new doubts about man's death. Until now he had vaguely believed that a man was simply extinguished once he was dead. Only those who believed in Christ would have their souls saved and so were able to go to heaven, and as for the others their lives would be extinguished along with their flesh. He did not even believe that a man was sent to hell if he had greatly sinned. He thought it obvious that Holy God would only take unto his Kingdom those who believed and followed him, but for some reason he found it hard to believe that He would punish unbelievers and send them to Hell. Thence he believed that there were only those who would receive salvation and go to heaven or those who would be extinguished.

But the people gathered here had completely different ideas. They thought that when someone died either his soul would go straight to the otherworld or was unable to do so. Since they did not really know about going to heaven or to paradise they summed all this up in one word: the otherworld.

It was good if one went straight to the otherworld, and if one did not things had gone wrong. But when things went wrong one did not cease to exist but the soul remained between this world and the otherworld and wandered about this middle ground until it fastened itself onto its living family or some other person. When the spirit of a dead man attached itself in this manner to a living man, this was called 'the ghost has possessed this man' or 'the ghost has fixed itself onto this man'. If this happens the man possessed will fall ill and the illness cannot be cured by medicine. Therefore a shaman performs an exorcism to get rid of the ghost of the dead man from a living man. A ghost which lodged itself in a host by accident was called 'Guest spirit' or 'tramp spirit' and could be removed by a simple exorcism but a ghost who sought its host having ties with them while still living, could not be governed by a simple exorcism, and had to be sent off to the otherworld by means of the 'O-gu' or the Great Rite.

Yongsul thought that all this in which the spectators held such firm belief, and which he had dismissed as mere superstition might have more sense in it than he had thought. After all was not the bible full of accounts of people possessed by ghosts. What were those ghosts? They were no different from the ghosts of which these people talked. Then did that not mean that such ghosts, whether in Israel or in our country, whether past or present, existed somewhere and sometime? Then this business of casting out ghosts was necessary. If a shaman could expel or send off to hell a ghost which was possessing someone that was something which was necessary and by that alone the shamans were blameless.

Thinking along these lines, Youngsul's heart suddenly

recoiled. The thought arose that even he who was so firm of faith could, in the midst of such a multitude of people, be swept away into thinking their thoughts and acknowledging their ways.

It was at that very instant. The noise of the crowd stopped at once and everyone turned their gaze to the offering table. Eulhwa had changed into a grey ceremonial robe of a princess and a tabard of tyrian purple. Holding a fan, she stood in front of the offering table.

Eulhwa snapped open her fan and began singing rapidly in one breath:

'Our Master Chung Mansu
Who fed fully the hungry
Who clothed warmly the naked
Who gave shelter and fare
To the homeless guest,
Who revered his parents
Who loved his brothers
And maintained good relations
With his kindred.
Who had a heart
Like unto the very Buddha
Now enters the afterworld.
Make way, clean the way!

Drum and cymbal and a tartar fiddle made together a loud racket, and when the narration ended the gong also was silent.

The crowd which had filled the entire garden was so silent that it seemed everyone was holding his breath. Two or three drum-beats broke the silence and Eulhwa's husky and sorrowful voice calmly rang out.

'Come out, Princess of the dead.'

At these words the crowd was so moved that there was an 'Aah' of admiration. Eulhwa turned and flashed her black eyes that shone like precious stones at the crowd, and as she raised her right hand high into the air her voice sticky as if it would leave stains on the skin rang out again:

Paridegi's father, he was
Emperor of the Greater Rite,

Paridegi's mother, she was
Consort of the Greater Rite.
Two years three years since the wedding
And still no signs of any baby
They go to offer sacrifice at the Holy Mountains
Mount Ying-Zhou and Mount Fang-Zhang
After three months and nine days of
Sacrificing to the Buddha,
She shows signs of carrying child.
She craves grapefruit, pomegranates,
Fairy peaches from paradise
Ten months gone and easy birth comes.
She prays to part the Gates of Hell
And Lo! It is a baby girl!
Swaddled in red silk she is named
Red Silk. When Red Silk is three years old
Again they go to famous mountains
Hundred days of prayer to Buddha.
From that month signs of carrying child
After ten months easy delivery
Praying to part the Gates of Hell.
Swaddled in white silk she is called
White Silk.
Again when she is three years old
Hundred days of prayer to Buddha
From that month signs of carrying child
Losing appetite in three months
The heels turning after nine months
After ten months easy delivery
Praying to part the Gates of Hell
Hell and damnation! Another daughter.'

The crowd burst into laughter.

The emperor's third baby girl was called Sam-Ye, the third
girl, the fourth was called Sa-Ye, the fourth girl, all the way
down to the eighth girl Pal-Ye, the eighth girl. Each time the
Emperor had another baby girl Eulhwa repeated the narration
and the same gestures but as if entranced the crowd just sighed
or burst into laughter.

'Listen to the words of the Emperor.

106

Eight times have I offered
Rite and Prayer to Buddha
By this eight daughters I have begotten
I have lost all hope!
Let us offer devotions once more
After that we call it quits.
Bathing in the Lower tub
Washing face in Middle tub
Cook sacrificial rice rinsed nine times
Rubbed his hands in prayer and bowed
With water from the upper tub.
From that month signs of carrying child
Actinia, wild grapes, apricots, pomegranates,
Fairy peaches from the Western Paradise
Bring them all and offer them to her
The child in her womb kicks and moves about
In a different fashion this time
And seems so much thicker
Come nine month it turns his heels
In the tenth month she is blessed with easy birth
Prayers are given to part the Gates of Hell
Oh, hell and damnation! another daughter!
Still lying down the Empress turns her back
On her royal consort
Listen to the words of his Imperial Majesty
If it is another daughter
Expose it on the pigweed patch
Who can dare disobey it
Since it is the imperial order
In tattered jacket and ragged skirt
Swaddled up in silken rags
She was abandoned on the pigweed patch.
Flap! Flap! Twin cranes are
Flying slowly down from heaven,
One bird cradles her, one wing supporting her
The other wing blankets her body
The other bird brings food for the little baby,
Carrying it on its beak,
Paridegi grows up in the pigweed patch.
The Emperor takes to bed with grave illness
He is stricken with the yellow jaundice, black jaundice,

His Lady Consort is possessed by a famished ghost
That eats whole cows for breakfast, lunch and dinner
Yet still cries out for more and more food
The best doctors in all of China are summoned
Hundred medicines are of no use
Soothsayers and fortune-tellers are summoned to divine a cure.
The first sign is cursed by heaven
The second sign is earth-cursed
The third sign says
Go and drink from the valley of Mt. Suyang
Whom shall we send to fetch this water?
Summoning eight daughters
Asking the first
Will you go, Red Silk?
Red Silk answers at once I cannot.
Why can't you go?
My son will soon be married
I cannot go
Asking the second
Will you go, White Silk?
I cannot go either, my daughter will soon be wed.
Will you go, Sam-Ye?
I cannot go either.
My parents-in-law have bad eyesight
Morning and Evening I must serve their meals.
Will you go, Sa-Ye?
I cannot go either
My late father-in-law's memorial day is nigh.
Will you go, O-Ye?
I cannot go either.
You too! Why?
Birth pangs are nigh upon me
That is why I cannot go.'

In such a manner did all eight daughters give excuses to avoid going to fetch the medicine. Whenever each daughter answered the crowd cried Aah! in lamentation or clicked their tongues scowling in indignation at the unfilial behaviours of daughters. When their lamentations and tongue-clickings subsided Eulhwa's sad voice quietly filled the air.

And when the eight daughters all went home
The Emperor said in a feeble voice
Listen neighbour wet nurse
Please fetch Paridegi from the pigweed patch
My illness is fast upon me
I wish to see her before I die
Neighbour nurse goes to the pigweed patch
Calling three times, Paridegi, Paridegi, Paridegi,
A girl as fair as the full moon looks out like the half moon
Who is looking for me?
There is no one who calls on me
Save a pair of cranes from heaven
The wet-nurse went to her and said
My child, Your father is the Emperor of the Great Rite
And your mother is the Empress of the Lesser Rite
She gave birth to nine daughters
And you are the ninth.
By Imperial Order you were abandoned in the pigweed
patch
Now the Emperor is sore afflicted
He wishes to see you before he dies.
Look at Paridegi
Alas! Cursed is my fate
Paridegi in the pigweed patch
Did I fall out of the sky
Did I spring forth from the earth
My parents who bore me
Abandoned me
So am I Paridegi the Abandoned One.
Now my parents are looking for me
There is no sea I will not cross
There is no mountain I will not climb
To be with them.
The maiden like the half moon
Rises forth like the full moon.
Paridegi returns home
Spreads a straw mat in the threshold
Bows three times three nice times
This unfilial Paridegi
Seeing you my parents
For the first time

Tears choke my throat
And I do not know what to say.
With shaking voice the Emperor calls her
Come here my child
You who were exposed on the pigweed patch
How you have grown!
We who abandoned you
Have no face to stand before you.
We are sore afflicted with a fatal illness
We shall soon die
Unless we drink of the spring in the valley of Mt. Suyang
We called all your eight sisters
All eight gave different excuses
Each one hurried back home
Now we are awaiting our death
We would like to see you one last time
Before we close our eyes forever.
Look at Paridegi
Her full moon face
Is washed with the rain of tears.
Father, Mother, I shall go
Alas, what ill fortune
To think I almost missed setting eyes upon my parents!
Painting her face black
Fastening an apron
Wearing a terrapin-bottle at her side
She goes in search of Mt. Suyang,
She does not know
East from West nor North from South
Goes as her feet guide her.
Washing woman beneath the rock
Across the stream
How do I get to the rocky valley of Mt. Suyang?
If you wash these black clothes white
I shall tell you how to get there.
Rolling the sleeves from
Her arms slender like a bamboo quiver
Washing black clothes white
Go and ask the builder of bridges over there
Oh, most noble bridge-builder
Which way to Mt. Suyang?

If you lay ninety-nine fathoms
Of an iron bridge
I shall show you.
She lays all ninety-nine fathoms of the iron bridge.
Go ask the builder of pagodas there.
Oh, most noble pagoda-builder,
Which way to Mt. Suyang?
If you stack all twelve stories of this pagoda
I shall show you.
Stacking all twelve stories
Go ask the washer of charcoal
Oh most noble charcoal washer
Which way to Mt. Suyang?
Wash this black charcoal white for me
And I will tell you.
She washes the charcoal white for him.
Go and ask the Buddhist Priest.
Great Priest, Great Priest,
Which way to Mt. Suyang?
Go there and ask the Maitreya
Oh Maitreya, Oh Maitreya
Where is Mt. Suyang?
Bear me nine sons
And I will tell you.
One year, two years, nine years pass
And she bears him all nine sons.
Oh Maitreya, Oh Maitreya,
Please tell me now.
Maitreya says
That is Mt. Suyang, over there
Small rivers, large rivers,
The endless deep blue sea
How can you cross them all?
Paridegi sits by the river
Legs outstretched, and laments aloud
Flap! Flap! two cranes fly down from heaven
And carry her to the other shore.
In the rocky valley of Mt. Suyang
Three nymphs from Mt. Suyang are bathing
Paridegi takes a nymph's garment
And hides under the thicket.

The first nymph comes out of the water
She smells sweat and human flesh
Elder nymphs put their clothes
And fly up to heaven
The youngest nymph looks here and there
To find her clothes.
Paridgei comes out of the thicket
Gives the nymph back her clothes
I too, I too am a woman.
Hearing Paridegi's words
Delighted the third nymph says
Paridegi of the pigweed patch
You too are a nymph.
Bring me back three bottles
In one bottle she puts
Water to enliven the blood
In another
Water to quicken the flesh
In the last
Water to restore breath
Taking leave of the nymph
She retreads the road she came on
Legs outstretched she sits a-crying
A turtle is sent from the dragon palace
Riding the turtle
She crosses the deep blue sea
Maitreya, Oh Maitreya
I want to go home
Listen to Maitreya
Since you are already late
Look at the sea before you go
Looking at it
Thousands of boats are
Returning from the netherworld.
What is that boat
In front of us
And roofed with straw
On that boat
Is a rich man
Who was viciously threshing his grain
When a poor man asked him for some

He threw him sheaf of straw
He shall go riding on that boat
Covered with straw to hell
What is that boat behind?
On that boat is one
Who glared and clicked his tongue
Before his parents
His eyes shall be gouged out
His tongue shall be pulled out
In hell.
And what is that boat?
On that boat is a wine seller
Who watered down his wine
He is going to deepest hell,
And what is that boat?
On that boat
Is a seller of straw shoes
Who sold his shoes for money
And did good deeds for other people
That boat is going up to heaven.
And what is that boat over there?
On that boat is a man
Who in this world
Fed the hungry
Clothed the naked
Shod the shoeless
Coming to the afterworld
He shall pile a heap of grain
Coins shall dangle from his jacket ribbons
From the flowerbed he shall be
Reincarnated in the Western Paradise.
Since I have seen everything
I think I shall go home now.
Listen to the Maitreya,
Take all your nine sons
Saying goodbye to the Maitreya
Carrying her nine sons
Quick, quick let us go
My mother and father are on the point of death
Hurrying back she finds
The Emperor and the Empress are dead

Waiting for their Paridegi
Both dying at the same hour
The funeral biers are leaving the palace
Listen to Paridegi
Oh Pallbearer, Oh pallbearer
Put it down the road
Put it up the road
I want to see the faces
Of my mother, of my father
Paridegi's eight sisters rush up to her
Slapping her on the right cheek on the left cheek
Where did you go that you come now?
We have kept vigil to the end
But get only fifteen plots of leech infested paddies
And fifteen plots of land fit for naught but dogshit.
Paridegi does not answer
Wiping her tears here and there
Clasping the coffin she laments
Opening the lid
She sees her aged parents
In their deathsleep.
She splashes the blood-enlivening water
And sweeps the blood-enlivening flower up and down
The colour returns to their faces
She splashes the flesh-quickening water
And sweeps the flesh-quickening flower up and down
Flesh regains its pinkish hue
She splashes the breath-reviving water
And sweeps the breath-reviving flower up and down
Her aged parents open their eyes at the same time
Rising up and saying:
Has our sleep been too deep
Am I dreaming, am I awake?
Who has saved we old parents
On our way to hell?
Who else but Paridegi
Paridegi takes them back home.
Look at the aged parents
Seating Paridegi's nine sons
On their laps at their sides
On both their knees.

Hooray, Hooray
What a sight to see
Paridegi, Paridegi, My Paridegi
Shall I give you all under heaven
Shall I give you all under earth
I don't want heaven I don't want earth
If there is one thing that I want
That is to feed well the hungry
Clothe well the naked
To give fare to those wandering penniless on the road.
For those spirits full of regrets and misery in the world
I wish to carve a way to the afterworld
Open the road to the Western Paradise
Open the road for their Reincarnation
Spirit of the deceased master!
May you flit on swift wings to the otherworld
Do not be broken-hearted
Nor let your heart nurse rancour
We pray to release you from your grief
And stuff your pockets full of travel money
So may you flit on
Swift wings to the otherworld!'

At this moment the three male shamans struck drum and
gong and cymbals and sang out in unison: 'May you flit on
swift wings to the underworld.'

The people assembled, sitting or standing in the garden
started to weep from when Paridegi appeared before her
parents, and when she stood in front of her parents having
brought them back to life with the medicine, everyone was
wiping their eyes on their sleeves or with their handkerchiefs.

What amazed Yongsul was not the fact that the entire
crowd was so moved, but that Wolhie seemed to understand
everything, looking on with a rapt air of attention. He asked:

'Did you hear everything?'

Wolhie nodded and said:

'I am going to draw Paridegi.' She had never before spoken
so clearly.

'How are you going to draw her?'

'I think I can see her.'

Wolhie again replied in a clear and distinct voice. At this

moment Lady Chung and her son the young Master Chung appeared before the offering table.

'Eulhwa!'

Lady Chung greeted Eulhwa patting her on the shoulder, and her son Chung Daeshik took out from his breast pocket three dark blue ten won notes and put two on the offering table and one in front of the male shamans. To pay a shaman even two hundred ryang was a huge sum of money, and on top of that to pay the male shamans separately was handsome treatment indeed. The people who had been watching this said:

'Eulhwa will become rich.'

Another added:

'Not one hundred but even two hundred ryang I would readily give to her.'

Chung Daeshik was thirty-seven years old. After having greeted the spectators he came out and looked around. When his glance alighted on Wolhie he stood motionless looking at her for a long time.

Chapter Twelve
WHAT THE WOMEN'S
OUTING BROUGHT

It was the Sunday, two days after the day of the exorcism at
Master Chung's house. As she had promised, Eulhwa left
Wolhie to Yongsul and allowed her to go to church. This
gesture was one purely to keep a promise and she did not
believe for a moment that there would be the least bit of
change as a result of this exercise. Yongsul himself could
foresee that given Wolhie's disability and her untrained mind
she would have difficulty in understanding the significance of
some parts of the service. Only, he believed in the power of
his weapons; his prayers for her and Wolhie's faith in him. The
result was more or less what Eulhwa had predicted and what
Yongsul himself had foreseen from the beginning.

That night, when Yongsul returned with Wolhie, Eulhwa
asked abruptly, 'Did our Dalhie say she liked Jesu worship?'

Yongsul could not answer straight away.

'She says she likes exorcisms better than Jesu worship,
doesn't she?

'Mother,' said Yongsul as if to stop what his mother was
saying.

'My dear son, please tell it as you saw.'

'But this was the first time Wolhie had been to church.'

'It was her first exorcism as well.'

'But she sees exorcisms all the time when she is at home.'

'You may have a point there. She has seen it at home and it
may have helped her, but still . . .'

'And there's one more thing. The church hall is divided into a men's section and a woman's section so that she was separated from me and I could not teach her anything.'

'Did our Dalhie go willingly to a place strange to her all by herself?'

'There was a woman I knew, the wife of Canon Kim, and I asked her to take care of Wolhie.'

'That's fine, but haven't you been able to talk to her on your way home?'

Yongsul was again lost for an answer.

'She said she didn't like it, didn't she?'

'No.'

'Then what?'

'She promised that she would attend church with me.'

'What is this? You mean our Dalhie said she would do Jesu worship with you?'

Yongsul did not reply.

'That's a lie, isn't it? I didn't promise you that I would allow you to deceive Dalhie into that Jesu worship, did I?'

'It is true that I did not get your prior permission.'

'Then does that mean our good and honest son has become a liar because of the Jesu demon?'

'Mother,' called Yongsul in a tone half imploring and half scolding.

'Why? Did I say anything wrong?'

'Mother, my love for Wolhie is next only to you. I only want Wolhie to grow up as a fine young lady and recover her speech as quickly as possible.'

'I can understand your stand but I can't allow you to lure our Dalhie into your Jesu worship.'

'Mother, let's leave it at that.'

'Leave it at that?'

Eulhwa remained staring at Yongsul, not quite satisfied, but seeing that he would not respond, she too turned away.

Having arrived at the present state of affairs, the experiment of Wolhie's preference between exorcism and the church service had to be declared a victory to Eulhwa. But unknown to all of them, the two outings which composed the experiment each brought about two quite unexpected results.

The first of these started when on the night of the exorcism,

Wolhie caught the eye of Chung Daeshik of the Chung household who had come out to greet the guests. When he spoke of her to his mother, the lady of the house, she replied, 'Now that you mention it. I was thinking of getting her a place somewhere because she seemed too precious to waste. If she pleases you so much, why don't you call her home and give her some odd jobs to do?' Her tone was that of implicit encouragement.

'That would be fine, mother.'

With this go-ahead from her son, the lady of the house went straight to Eulhwa and made known her wishes.

Eulhwa gave her answer without a moment's hesitation with her face beaming with joy.

'If our Dalhie pleased Master Chung so much, what could be better?'

Usually, the best that could be hoped for a shaman's daughter was for her to marry another shaman's son, or otherwise become a small shaman without a helper (husband). A shaman's daughter to become a Kisaeng girl or for her to enter the house of a nobleman's house or that of a rich household as a concubine was a prize beyond reasonable expectation.

The lady of the house also seemed satisfied and said, 'I'll be honest with you Eulhwa, but with her looks, were she born to a respectable household, she would have been a candidate for the King's palace itself.'

At this Eulhwa joined in and said, 'Didn't I tell you? When I had her, I saw the princess of a moon god.' Not being able to resist she showed off.

After the lady had left, Eulhwa turned to Wolhie and advised her of her new duties.

'My princess, dear princess,

My treasure chest, my dear treasure chest.

In a very short space of time you are going to be a bride of Master Chung. So from now on, forget about the Jesu house and just stay home making yourself beautiful.'

As for the other result of Wolhie's outing, that is, at the church, it was a matter which affected Yongsul more than it did Wolhie.

That day when Wolhie was taken to the church, Canon Kim's wife had taken her to a corner of the front row of the congregation on the women's side, and the eyes of everyone there came to be focused on Wolhie.

Ordinarily when a newcomer appeared in church, many eyes would move to that direction since the church was quite new and any member of the church was received with gratitude and welcome, but the attention that Wolhie attracted was something beyond the ordinary. The reason, apart from the fact that she was a new member of the church was that her appearance and her dress was so beautiful.

To speak of the dress of the women present at the church, most wore the white *chima* and *jogori*, with the exception of some young wives or unmarried women who would wear a black *chima* or rarely, a light jade-colour one. But this strange young woman had on a bright green *chima* and *jogori*. On top of that, her movement was that of a willow branch and her face that of jade, so that it was hardly surprising that she stole the show.

According to Canon Kim's wife who told Yongsul of the things said about her, there were whispers of, 'She doesn't seem like someone who could eat earthly food and live on the face of the earth,' or, 'An angel would run away after seeing her for shame,' and 'I can't tell if she's a spirit or a human being,' and 'I don't know if I'm dreaming or if I'm awake.'

This kind of fuss soon brought Yongsul in the picture and in no time, it reached the stage when the fact that the mother of the brother and sister was Eulhwa became known. Although Yongsul prided himself in being a devout Christian, emancipated from the bonds of his birth, there was no reason why he would like his identity as a shaman's son being made public, and that was why he had only told his teacher Park Kunshik about his background. But now, with just one appearance of Wolhie, everything about his past and his origin became known to all.

Although it was not something he had wanted and certainly not one that he could be proud of, he consoled himself that the truth being the truth it would have had to come out into the open sooner or later. But the saga did not end there. It gave itself another twist and reached the point where the very birth of Yongsul was brought into the question and also the talk of the entry of his name into a family register came into being.

It was twelve days after Wolhie's eventful visit to the church and so the Friday of the week after. Yongsul received a word from Master Park and visited him. Park, in a voice even more solemn than usual, said, 'The reason I wanted to see you was nothing other than . . .' Stretching out the introduction, continued Park gravely.

'It is an unexpected turn of events and something which affects you to a great extent . . .'

Yongsul assumed that he was going to talk to him about the new unfavourable atmosphere of the church since his identity was revealed. He hurried Park along.

'Master, I fear nothing except the wrath of the Almighty. Please tell me what it is.'

'Have you heard the story about Bamnamutgol (chestnut tree village)?'

'No sir, I don't think so. This is the first time I have heard of it.'

At this reply from Yongsul, Elder Park put on a puzzled face and stared at him for a while after which he said, 'Don't you even know that Bamnamutgol was your birthplace?'

'No sir, I only heard that we moved from Yokchon to Jatshil.'

'That's right. You were born at Yokchon but a little while before that your father lived in the chestnut tree village. That is to say, your father is an inhabitant there.'

'Sir, this is the first time I have heard of this.'

Yongsul replied with his face blushing and in a voice seemingly mixed with tears.

'Really?'

Elder Park, taken aback, sat looking at Yongsul and finally spoke again.

'Your father is an inhabitant of the chestnut tree village, a man named Lee Sungchool.'

'But, sir!'

'Just listen a little longer.'

Park waited a moment for Yongsul's excitement to cool down and then spoke again.

'The mother and wife of your real father have been members of our church for some time. They of course had no idea of who you were until that Sunday when your sister came to church, do you remember? Well, from then everything about your origin became known.'

'I am sorry for all the trouble I have caused, sir.'

Yongsul drooped his flushed face and only managed to say these words and that, with tears in his voice.

'As you said a moment ago, there is nothing to fear except the wrath of God. Relax and listen to the rest of what I have to say. But as your father and his wife had an only daughter, who got married and left home, there is no one that could be called a blood relative left in the house. It seems that the two ladies, after seeing you, mentioned the matter when they went home. Soon after, your father came to visit me with Canon Kim, who incidentally is my cousin and apparently a friend of your father's.'

Park stopped what he was saying for a moment to observe Yongsul's face, but Yongsul's face, as red as a carrot, was held low and no sound came from him. Elder Park continued.

'And what he says is that if the family line comes to an end in his generation his household would be closing its shutters and he would be a sinner in the eyes of his ancestors. He is very insistent in seeing you.'

Yongsul was aware that Elder Park was studying his face to observe his mood, but he remained silent with his face towards the floor. Park, in a softer voice than before spoke to him again.

'It seems there isn't a suitable candidate for an adopted son, either. Of course, the knowledge of there being a son, a true son related by blood would rule out such a course anyway. So when he heard that you and I were close, he came to me to ask me to put in a few words on his behalf. If your father was free to have his way, – of course, your opinion would have to come into it as well – what he wants is to meet you, receive you as his son, record you in the family register and make you carry on the family line.'

Elder Park stopped there, apparently thinking that he had transmitted the message adequately enough and went back to staring at Yongsul for an answer. He obviously thought there would be an answer from him now. But Yongsul remained with his face dropped to the ground and did not even move.

'Knowing how sensible you are, I know you will handle this matter well, but in my opinion, I think it would be better if you took the opportunity. Then your father would follow you in coming to church, and . . . isn't that so?'

Yongsul quietly turned his face to the left. It was a motion designed to hide his tears from the master, but it became the impulse that broke loose the torrent of tears that he had barely managed to hold in. His shoulders, turned to his left, shook up and down conspicuously and Park only then realized that the reason Yongsul had remained so quiet with his head down was to restrain himself from bursting into tears.

When the sobbing had stopped, Yongsul managed to squeeze a tearful sentence in.

'I'm sorry Elder Park.'

'Nonsense. It's only natural for someone in your position.'

Park wanted to comfort him a little more but could not think of anything more to say.

Yongsul, as if he had forgotten that the master was waiting for his reply, sat there with his red eyes glued to the floor. Park deduced that it was he who had to speak again.

'As two Christians and furthermore as two human beings, I have regarded you as my son. Please don't get me wrong. Up till now, I didn't know your surname and you have lived without knowing your surname. Now, you have discovered it. You are by all standards a Lee. Take your surname. I know that someone like you who lives by God's will, will not desire the ephemeral vanities of this world like wealth, fame, and high position, but even so, to live in this world without knowing your own surname is unthinkable. You are a Lee. Have your surname,' said Park, as if to hasten Yongsul's decision.

'Ever since I arrived here, I have received your support as I did from the missionaries when I was in Pyongyang. In such a position, I would not dare take anything you say lightly, but I have a mother. Though she is a low and shameful shaman, she still is my mother. Even if the story about chestnut tree village is true, I think it better were I to ask her opinion before I rush into anything.'

'That is true. That would be the right order to handle it.'

The Elder replied in a low voice and slowly nodded his head.

Chapter Thirteen
SURNAME REGAINED

When Yongsul related this incident to Eulhwa she just
listened with pouted lips and replied abruptly.

'Yes, it was at chestnut tree village,' and she added, 'that is
the reason why I never go there to perform any rites.'

When Yongsul looked at her as if to ask if that was the
only reason, she added,

'I was carrying you inside me when they cast me out of the
village.'

'Cast you out?'

Pouting her lips again, Eulhwa nodded a couple of times
and spoke slowly.

'At that time, my mother, that is to say your grandmother,
barely eked out a living by doing other people's housework
around the village. When I became pregnant the whole village
cut us dead, averting their eyes when they passed us by
because an unmarried girl had become heavy with child. Not
only that, his family begged us to leave, saying that I would
smash a fellow's chances of finding a wife. So since there was
nothing else to do, we left for Yokchon village where we had
lived before.'

'What does it mean, "smash a fellow's chances of getting
married"?'

Such were the words of those who would not even stop to
think of the pregnant Eulhwa as a possible wife.

'Was there no gossip later on?'

124

'When he tried to get married after all that, there was so much trouble that on two occasions his marriage talks were broken off. He had such a hard time that when we moved from Yokchon to Jatshil to the town wandering from village to village not once did they make any effort to know whether we were dead or alive and not once did they try to find out whether you were still living or long dead. To this day they pretend that nothing ever happened, having swept everything under the carpet.'

Eulhwa's voice smouldered with resentment.

'What are your thoughts on the matter, mother?'

Eulhwa did not answer Yongsul's question.

'Did you not say that the wife saw you when she came to worship Jesus. Those bitches would not have been able to see you had it not been for that Jesus and would not in their wildest dreams have dared to think of you.'

Yongsul did not think that this even merited a reply and so kept his peace. Furious, Eulhwa exploded:

'I cannot even hold my head up before the Spirit for shame that you have been possessed by this Jesus devil, and to think that you will fall down in the Jesus pit together with those bitches makes my skin crawl. Soon Dalhie will be married into the Chung household and I shall have no one left. What shall then become of me?'

'Did you say Dalhie will go to the Chung household?'

'Yes, the young master was smitten by Dalhie the very first time he set eyes on her according to the wife of their household. He would like to install her as part of the family.'

'And so did you agree to this, mother?'

'Well, you don't think that anything better will come our way, do you?'

'. . . .'

'Truly we are blessed in our Dalhie, so fair of face that she could stand compare with the nymph of Mount Wushan. In our situation to hope for such a position for a daughter would be like a commoner becoming a queen.'

'But mother, in what status will our Wolhie go?'

'She will go as Master Chung's wife, what else?'

'How can she go as Master Chung's wife, when he has already a wife and child?'

'Because of your Jesus business you know nothing of how

the world goes round. When a rich man or a nobleman reaches thirty he must keep a concubine for fear of losing face. It is because Master Chung is of such mild temper and because he and Dalhie are a pair of star-crossed lovers that he has thus delayed matters.'

'But mother, don't you feel sorry for Dalhie?'

'Why, feel sorry for her when things are going so well for her?'

'Don't you feel sorry for her who is to become another's plaything?'

'What nonsense are you spouting? How dare you call her a plaything, she who will become a wife in that household?'

'If you give Wolhie as concubine to Master Chung who clearly has a wife and child, will not Wolhie be something that is superfluous? Wellborn or illborn, should we let her pick and choose one who will be her mate and hers alone?'

'Since you started doing this Jesus business, you say a lot of rubbish. A nymph of Wusham has found her fated lover and all you can talk of is "plaything" or "superfluous", words picked to make my lungs burst with rage. Clever though you are you know less about life than I, your mother. Everyone has his lot and station in life. Who would take the likes of me as a second, nay even a third wife? Though our Dalhie be as fair as the nymph of Wushan, would a farmer wed her and live together off the land? Would a merchant take her to cry wares together in the market place? Would a king take her and enthrone her as his queen? If you want to make such foolish talk then don't you go any more to do this Jesus business. That someone as clever as you, my son, should rattle off such nonsense must be because that Jesus devil has possessed you.'

When she was like this Yongsul could not put a word in edgeways. Words, however reasonable, were useless. Besides, Yongsul understood that such words would only fan her anger.

But Yongsul resolved henceforth that he would fight to the bitter end to prevent Wolhie from being sent as a concubine to Master Chung's. He went to see Elder Park and, without hiding a single thing, told him of Eulhwa's intention and of his resolve to keep Wolhie to the end.

'Master Lee.'

126

Elder Park called thus and without saying a word about Wolhie, continued.

'Since your mother has also acknowledged it, it has become clear that without a single doubt your natural father is Lee Sungchool. You do not know what a source of frustration it has been to me not to know your true surname. Whether you decide to live in the Lee household or not, from now on I shall call you "Master Lee". As for my opinion on where you should live, I think that you should not be overly concerned about your mother or sister but you should go and live in the house of your natural father. Do you understand?'

'Your Worship, how could I even for a moment dare think lightly of your words, but, your worship, I had a purpose in coming back to my village. This was to spread the word of God to my poor mother and sister and to make them into those who could walk before God with me. Under the pastor's loving kindness and teaching I spent many days so full of bliss, but I came back, not being able to endure the thought that my mother and my sister would be wandering in the dark valley of evil, enslaved by a vile ghost. I resolved that I would fear no hardship nor flinch from any suffering and that I would not retreat till I could raise a paean of victory in praise of our Lord. And as I thought that this would be in accord with the wishes of the reverend pastor who sheweth me loving kindness and grace abounding, I entreated him and returned, having barely received his permission. How then could I thus forsake my mother and my sister and leave for other parts?'

'I am thankful for your thoughts and find your resolve most admirable, but to go and live in the house of your natural father would not mean forsaking your mother and sister. Though you move to chestnut tree village you can always visit them whenever it takes your fancy. If it be necessary can you not live here with your mother and sister and stay with your natural father from time to time. On that matter it will be the easiest of things for me to get your natural father's permission. Hence, since it is something that they want most dearly in their hearts let you first give consent and go into their house to pay your respects, then let you decide according to your circumstances whether to stay here in this village or to live there and drop in occasionally. I think that it would be more effective for you to stay there and drop in occasionally to coax her gently than stay here and constantly fight. What do you think?'

Yongsul was silent and could not give a quick reply. In neither case would he be able to receive his mother's consent.

'Do you find even that too difficult?'

'Sir, it differs not from the other proposal in that I trust in both cases overcome my mother's apposition.'

'But it is not impossible, is it? You did not choose to believe in God with the permission of your mother. You need not have her permission in everything that you do. Be firm and stiffen your resolve.'

'I shall do as you say, sir.' Yongsul had finally affirmed his decision.

'Thank you. You should do as I said.' Elder Park looked gratified.

But Yongsul did not wait to hear these words but stood up immediately. Taken aback, Elder Park watched Yongsul with a disconcerted expression on his face.

Facing the corner of the room, Yongsul knelt, then closed his eyes and bowed his head. He seemed to be praying. Elder Park found it hard to understand why he should pray in such a disturbing manner. Having finished prayer, Yongsul again turned toward Elder Park, and still kneeling, said:

'I hope that you will continue to watch over me and give prayer to Lord that I shall not weaken in my resolve to fulfil my purpose.'

His voice was higher than usual and there was a queer gleam of excitment playing over his features.

It was the evening of the following Sunday. Yongsul had finished the afternoon service and was alighting onto the threshold, when the wife of Deacon Kim rushed up to him as if she had been waiting all along and lightly caught his sleeve. As he turned his head towards her, she also turned and pointed with her finger to a shortish old lady with a wrinkled face, saying:

'Chestnut tree village . . .'

It seemed she meant the granny from chestnut tree village. Next to the old lady was a woman in her forties, of darkish complexion.

Yongsul stood there not knowing what to do, with a slight smile on his puckered face. Without hesitating the old lady

128

quickly seized him by the sleeve and stroking his arm said:

'How comely you are! Is it because you are of my blood that you stand out so from the common herd?'

So saying she turned to the woman next to her, who responded with a smile on her darkish face.

'Of course, mother. Is this not all due to our Lord's grace?'

So this old lady was the mother of Lee Sungchool, and the other woman his wife. The granny stepped right up to Yongsul and looked at him straight in the face.

'You are of my blood, how can you think of going anywhere else? Come, let us go to chestnut tree village.'

So saying he tugged his sleeve. His sleeve still caught by the old lady Yongsul smiled a bitter smile and stood there, hesitating.

'I too have heard of chestnut tree village from Elder Park and had the intention of visiting you within the next few days.'

Then the woman stepped right next to the granny and putting her hand on top of hers, said:

'What welcome tidings! My, how nice that would be! All is thanks to the Lord's grace,' and looking at the granny again she said.

'Mother, sad though it is to leave this, let us go home. However dear blood kinship may be is it not right to make some preparations for a first visit? Let us prepare some food tomorrow and invite him the day after.'

Granny could not keep her eyes off Yongsul's face.

'Of course, of course, we will hold a feast, we must hold a feast, a huge feast. It must be by the grace of our Lord, for without His grace whence could come such a grandson, so handsome that he outshines the moon?'

She went on like this for a while, and then for no particular reason she clicked her tongue and dabbed her tears with her sleeve. Yongsul also felt rather sad and gently patted granny on the back.

'Grandmother, please put a stop to all this and please go home. I shall come and visit you be it tomorrow or the day after.'

Thus did he comfort her, in words of the local dialect.

Chapter Fourteen
IN THE FATHER'S HOUSE

Chestnut tree village was about four kilometres south east of the town. Mountains arose behind it and in front stretched a broad plain. A small stream ran across the face of the plain.

When Yongsul arrived at his father's house with Elder Park, there were already gathered Deacon Park, who was the Elder's younger cousin, an old man who claimed to be the uncle of Yongsul's father, and several female kin.

The house was divided into a main building and an outhouse. In the main building were the living room, a small room, a wooden floor running in between them and in the extreme west a kitchen. His father, his father's uncle and the other male guests were gathered in the living room, whilst the womenfolk were sitting in the smaller room and the wooden floor. The outhouse consisted of a storeroom, a room for the farmhand and a stable which also served as an open shed. At the very end stood a latrine facing the compost heap.

Yongsul entered the courtyard, following Elder Park. Immediately Deacon Park, who was the Elder's younger cousin sprang out and led them to the living room. As Elder Park and Yongsul's father had already met, when they stepped onto the threshold, Yongsul's father came out of the room to greet them. As his gaze turned from Elder Park to Yongsul, Yongsul did not miss the joyful smile that spread from the corners of his father's eyes and mouth.

They entered the room and sat facing the host. Elder Park

looked around those who had gathered and greeted them and said pointing to the host.

'This is your father. Bow and greet him.'

Yongsul stood up and bowed gravely. As he regained his place, squatting on his haunches, Elder Park again pointed to the old man who sat next to his father saying:

'And now to this elder . . .'

Yongsul bowed as before and sat down. Elder Park explained.

'He would be your paternal grandfather's second cousin.'

Not knowing exactly what that meant, Yongsul just sat there nodding his head. When Yongsul had more or less finished greeting those assembled, the old lady he had seen that day at the church entered the room and sat herself down in front of the door sill, saying:

'I too would like to receive a bow from my grandson.'

Everyone present, both those in the room and those in the floor outside, roared with laughter. Then the host Lee Sungchool arose and said:

'Well, mother, if you must get your bow come and sit here and get it.'

And he pulled the old lady by the arm to the place of honour where he was sitting. Having received her bow, she continued:

'There's no accounting for blood. Do you know when I first saw him at the church, tears sprang to my eyes.' Wiping her eyes again with her sleeve, she then called out to the floor.

'Daughter-in-law, let you come into this room as well.'

A woman's voice answered in the floor outside.

'Of course, he must bow to his mother. Has Hanshil-taek (the woman from Hanshil) gone somewhere?'

Hanshil-taek mounted the floor from the courtyard and politely refused, saying:

'Did I not see him at the church? It doesn't matter if I don't get a bow.'

But as if she could not overcome the protestations of 'How could you?' and 'Oh, but you must', the dark-complexioned Hanshil-taek gave way and received Yongsul's bow sitting next to the old lady, then as if she felt bashful she looked back once or twice at the man, her husband's paternal cousin, and said:

'Truly the Lord's grace has no bounds.'

She then rose and went out, saying:

'We shall bring in the food shortly.'

Whilst Yongsul was kowtowing in obeisance to his elders, the women had been watching this scene from the floor. With faces moved by emotion they laughed or clicked their tongues or shook their heads, and when Hanshil-taek came out they all rushed to touch her sleeve or hands saying:

'Hanshil-taek has finally gotten what she has yearned for.'

When the tables full of food were brought in Deacon Park turned to the host and the old man and said:

'On such a blessed day, let first give thanks to the Lord before we break our fast.'

The elderly relative kept his peace as if he did not really want to concern himself with such matters. The host looked across at Deacon Park and said:

'Didn't I tell you to handle things as you saw fit?'

Deacon Park turned to Elder Park and requested.

'Elder Brother, please guide us in our prayer.'

Elder Park closed his eyes as if he had been waiting for this cue and started praying.

'Our Father who art in heaven, on this day through thy grace there has come to pass in this household as great a blessing that man can hope for. Mr. Lee Sungchool, of this household has finally come face to face with his only flesh and blood, of whom he had no news until this day. He can now continue ever more his line through his own natural and true son. What greater blessing can man or of woman hope for? Lord, we know that all this hath come to pass through thy grace.

'As for young Master Lee Yongsul, as thy dearly beloved lamb so precious a youth to thy church of Kyungju, and who is to this family as dear as a flower that flowereth from a dead branch, who hath on his shoulders the solemn duty of carrying on forever the lineage of this house. Our Father, who art the Lord, give unto this household even more of thy blessing and look over things with the might of thy holy spirit so that Master Lee Yongsul, as the natural son of this house shall be filial son to his parents and live in peace with his kin and neighbours, and that thy holy spirit make it pass that this whole family hold hands and sing hymns before thee. That this shall come to pass we sincerely, sincerely beg of thee. We beg thee in the name of Jesus Christ our Lord. Amen.'

Whilst Elder Park was praying, Lee Sungchool sat still with his eyes resting on the meal table but the old man, his cousin, looked sideways once or twice at his cousin. Finally, as if he could no longer stand it, seized his tobacco pouch and twice made as if to stand up. On each occasion Deacon Park who sat next to him prevented him from rising by tugging at his clothes, but in doing so he had to stealthily lower his eyes and turn his gaze to the old man.

When they had finished praying Hanshil-taek brought in a bowl of sweet rice wine on a tray and giving it to the old man, asking his permission.

'Elder cousin, on this day I shall serve sweet rice wine instead of the cloudy rice wine.'

But the old man took his bowl with a sour face and just set it in front of him, not even condescending to look in her direction.

But on the table fruit and cakes and greens and cuts of pork and chicken were piled high on big plates and several plates of fried or grilled fish had also been placed. So all in all as everyone started helping themselves each according to his taste, so there was no need in particular for anyone to pay attention to anyone else. But as if she was still troubled by the old man, Hanshil-taek brought in a small plateful of sautéed chicken giblets and offered it to him, saying:

'Elder cousin, please try some of this.'

As if he had been appeased the old man stared at her full in the face for a while then took the offered dish. He put it in the corner of the table and took up his chopsticks. Then Hanshil-taek beamed as if with relief and turned, saying:

'Elder cousin, please eat to your heart's content.'

'Hallelujah, Hallelujah!'

Out on the wooden floor Granny was singing a hymn. Brandishing a piece of chicken in one hand and cakes in the other she was lifting her shoulders in time to her song. But seeing that there was no one in the crowd of women, in the small room and the floor who could join her, Hanshil-taek who was still holding the tray with the wine bowl on it, added her voice to her mother-in-law's hymn.

'. . . . And with His blood my sins are washed away.'

On seeing this all the women simultaneously burst into laughter. Not only was it amusing to see Hanshil-taek, normally so meek and retiring, sing hymns holding a rice bowl in one hand, the sight of a daughter-in-law so behaving with the intention of adding her voice to her mother-in-law's solo seemed to please them. Encouraged by the women's laughter mother-in-law and daughter-in-law continued singing their hymn.

'Hallelujah, Hallelujah,
As I believe in Jesus
With His Blood He
Redeemeth me.'

As the duet thus ended one woman cried out in a voice thick with emotion.

'Where in the world could one find a sight to compare with this?'

But before the other woman could agree Hanshil-taek's voice broke in. Still holding the bowl of wine and looking down at her mother-in-law who was still brandishing her cake and rocking her shoulders, she repeated the end of the hymn over and over again.

'Hallelujah
Hallelujah
He redeemeth me
He redeemeth me.'

Then her neighbour the widow said to the old lady of the date-field who sat next to her.

'Lady, you've just heard Hanshil-taek's song, haven't you. Did she not say that believing in the Christ she has found and offered a son, and has washed away her sin of not having borne sons to her husband. Did she not say that she has redeemed her sins?'

The old lady of the date-field nodded:

'Yes, now that I think upon it it seems to mean that.'

This conversation soon spread to the other women.

'They say that at last Hanshil-taek has completely washed away her sin of not having borne sons.'

So they all murmured amongst themselves, nodding their heads.

In the living room Lee Sungchool was talking to Yongsul.

'Why are you not eating? Does the food not please you?'

134

'No sir, I am helping myself.'

So saying Yongsul picked up a peach.

From the beginning images of his mother and his younger sister kept flickering in front of his eyes so that he found it hard to eat. In his heart he would have liked to leave together with Elder Park when the meal had come to an end, but since Elder Park had instructed him that whatever happened he just spend the first night at his father's, Yongsul could do nothing but harden his heart and endure.

It had been arranged that Yongsul sleep in the small room. That night, his grandmother came to him and said:

'If you don't mind I shall sleep in this room together with you. What do you say? Do you mind? If you don't like it I can sleep alone in the hall or I can sleep with your father in the living room.'

'Do as you like grandmother, I don't mind either way.'

'Oh, thank you. I don't know what I would have done if you had refused.' She said, stroking his cheek.

That night after they had put their heads to pillow, grasping Yongsul's hand as tightly as she could, she began to relate the story of what had happened.

'In the beginning your mother who bore you lived right next to us, in the house that lay to the east of ours. Now there is a wall that divides the two houses, but at that time there was but a hedge separating the two houses so that one could look in and see what was happening in the other house.'

Since his father's invitation Yongsul had also vaguely heard this story from his mother but he held his peace. Grandmother continued her story.

'At that time your mother was sixteen and your maternal grandmother was a young widow of some thirty-five years of age, who lived by doing chores for other houses, being hired out for the day by this house, then by another house on the next day. In such a situation they could not but leave the village when your mother became heavy with child. Had we known that things would have turned out in this way we would have prevented your mother from leaving by main force and married her off to your father, but who can know what the future will bring? Though it may cause you rancour to hear such a thing at that time and in such a situation we could do nothing else.'

'Grandmother, what use is it to regret things past?'

'It is because as I stand before you I am overcome by shame and guilt. Even after that on occasion I thought of you but when I heard that your mother had become a shamaness I did not dare think of looking for you and now through the grace of our Lord has not blood kin found blood kin again?'

After she had related the tale she paused for a long while and spoke again.

'The mother of this house is also good and righteous beyond bounds. Her only fault is that she is barren of sons. Apart from that she is blameless. Think of her as the mother that bore you.'

'Grandmother, are we not all a family which reveres and worships our Lord the Father? This day when you and mother were singing Hallelujah's on the floor, I wept to myself in secret. For more than the mother who bore me and raised me amongst insult and suffering I felt that she here were my true mother and you my true grandmother. Is this not because we are one as a family which worships and reveres God our Father? But not even for an instant can I forget my mother who bore me.

'Grandmother, if I could through my efforts release her from this shaman devil that posseses her and make things come to pass that she believes in Jesus Christ our Lord. If I could do such a thing gladly would I exchange my life for it.'

And so saying and being full of a sudden fervour he grasped the thin hands of his grandmother that lay at his side.

'Yes, yes, go to sleep now.' Spoke his grandmother in a throaty voice as if she had been asleep and had just woken up.

The next day after breakfast Yongsul went to town to the house of Elder Park to pay his respects and then returned home. Mother was already out and Wolhie was alone painting a crimson demon. He watched this scene for a moment thinking that the crimson demon made a marvellous contrast with her willow green skirt and jacket, then asked.

'What is that picture?'

'Mother said for her exorcism rites . . .'

Putting her brush down she looked at Yongsul and answered him thus. She meant that this picture would be used at mother's exorcism rites.

Looking at Wolhie's face as she spoke Yongsul was seized by pity and chagrin for her. Eyes closed he turned and faced the wall biting his lips to check the grief that rushed to his throat. It was a feeling like a sudden and violent spasm of nameless grief and sorrow and longing all mingled into one. He wiped his tears with his sleeve and took out a bible from his breast to calm himself.

Meanwhile Wolhie who had cleared paint and brush away to one corner of the room touched Yongsul lightly on the arm saying:

'Please don't cry, Elder Brother.'

Full of surprise at how she had guessed his sorrow he clasped her and sat down, saying:

'Sit there, Wolhie!'

Still holding onto her wrist he asked.

'Wolhie, can you put your trust in me, your brother?'

Looking at Yongsul's face with her starlike eyes, she nodded.

'You must believe in God together with me, your brother.'

Yongsul's voice started to shake for no reason at all. He continued.

'I wish to marry you to a fellow believer in Christ.'

Seeing that Wolhie would not be able to follow a long speech he cut short his words thus.

'Marry?'

'That's right. You must marry a husband that I choose for you.'

Wolhie was silent. For some reason she shook her head from side to side. But since there was something that he had to tell her he decided to let things go at that.

'Wolhie, you must not go to the Chung household.'

'To the Chung household?'

'That's right. Master Chung has both wife and son and daughter. If you go as his wife you will buy other people's hatred and hear God's reproof. You know this, don't you?'

Wolhie was silent. As if she did not understand him well she just stared at him foolishly.

'Even if mother tries to send you off to Master Chung you must not go. Say that you cannot. I will guard you. Do you understand?'

Still silent, Wolhie nodded. She nodded, not because she understood his words but because simply she wanted to listen to his urgent plea.

Yongsul also did not think that she understood enough of what he said. But he believed that she knew well enough that she must not go as wife to the Chung household. Still holding onto her wrist he started to pray.

'Oh God our Father who saveth the pitiful and helpeth the weak, help our pitiful and miserable younger sister. This pitiful is possessed of a spirit and does not yet have the power of speech, and is fated to be dragged to the place of evil by our mother who is possessed of a dread spirit. Oh God our Father, please help my mother and my younger sister to escape from the clutches of this dread spirit. We beg thee to chase away this spirit with thy holy fire so that we may together go before thee and sing hymns . . .'

At this moment Eulhwa opened the door and entered the room. Yongsul had vaguely heard someone entering but since he could not suddenly break off his prayer she had entered while he was in the process of finishing his prayer.

Yongsul quickly finished his prayer and looking up at his mother he quickly retrieved the bible which lay in front of him and put it back inside his shirt next to his breast. Eulhwa, who had stood still in front of the door sill watching her son's actions with blazing black eyes that glittered with rage, cast a glance around the room, and her gaze alighting on Wolhie's drawing utensils put aside in one corner of the room she asked as if to pick a fight.

'Is it this Jesus devil's doing that prevented our Dalhie from finishing her picture?'

Her face and voice were full of venom and rage. Smiling, Yongsul answered his mother in a sweet and modest voice.

'Mother, I asked our Wolhie to stop painting because I wanted to talk to her.'

'What talk? Did you tell her that the picture repelled you intensely?

'No, mother. I did but ask what the picture was.'

'Then what did our Dalhie say?'

'She just said it was to be used at your exorcism ceremony.'

As if appeased by her son's frank answer Eulhwa said:

'That's right, it's what I had asked our Dalhie to do for me.

I asked her to draw me a Jesus devil. I asked her to draw it bright red since the Jesus devil is red . . . . So when you saw it, it must have made your stomach turn.'

'Mother, I found it rather grotesque but it did not make my stomach turn.'

'My good son, you too must slowly get rid of this Jesus demon.'

'Mother, our Lord Jesus is not a demon but the Son of God. He is a holy one who came down to Earth as the Son of God and died on the cross to atone for the sins of mankind. Through Christ's spilled blood God forgives us our sins, saves our souls and lets us live forever in heaven.'

Seeing that Eulhwa's rage had subsided a little thus did he try to explain the essential teachings of the Christian creed. Eulhwa listened as if she marvelled at his words, then going as far as to smile said:

'Well, that's really interesting. So that's why the fools flock to do the Jesus.'

'Mother, it is not because they are fools but because it is the Truth that they believe in.'

'Truth? You listen to me. Say that you are right and that Jesus is not a demon but a man. Whether he be the son of God or the son of the Great Spirit is he not a man since he was born on this earth? Since he is a man will he not die? He has died and become a demon. So that's why he is the Jesus demon. The reason why you go around blowing your trumpet is because you are possessed by a demon.'

'Mother!'

'Yes, listen to me. You said that if you believe in this Jesus demon that your souls will be saved and that you will go to heaven, didn't you? You would like this to happen, wouldn't you? But who has seen this and who has gone to heaven and come back? So you can't know for sure, can you? No listen. There is a way of finding this out for sure on this earth. People call me the shaman, don't they? You too have received many slights and harboured much grief for being the son of a shaman. But that is one thing that I know for sure. Listen to this. When a man dies he becomes a ghost. The priests in the temple go straight to the other world, but ordinary mortals often go to the realm of ghosts which lies in between this world and the otherworld. Moreover those who were drowned or were stabbed to death or hanged themselves or died of smallpox live in the realm of ghosts wandering around the very edge of this world. If you die of some sickness or if you have too much sorrow and resentment in this world this also happens. Such ghosts attach themselves to those whom they have known in this life, or to anyone who is feeble-minded and weak in body. Then such a person will become bedridden with some illness or go mad or he may fail in business or put torch to his own house. He then dies. Such a sickness you cannot cure with medicines but only a spirit child can cure it. People call the spirit child a shaman and treat her with all sorts of contempt but this is because the fools do not know what a spirit child is. A spirit child is the son and the daughter of the Great Spirit. You said that Jesus is the son of God, well that is more or less the same as saying our spirit child, the ordinary shaman, is the son of the Great Spirit.'

'Mother,' Yongsul interrupted her. 'Please don't confuse Our Lord Jesus with the shaman.'

He protested solemnly using the Seoul speech which in the heat of anger he had reverted to unbeknown to himself. Full of anger he tried to get up. But Eulhwa reproached him in a calm and quiet voice.

'So now even you despise me as the others do.'

'No, mother, it is not that I despise you but that I hate the ghost that is inside you.'

'What? That is the same as your despising your Jesus ghost or your God ghost. Listen. Did you say that he cured those possessed of ghosts? That's it. Curing those possessed of ghosts. To this day I have been curing those who were possessed by ghosts and about to die or had their livelihood ruined as a result. By the Great Rite or by the Rite of Banishment I part the ghost from his host and send him to the otherworld. Think how indignant and resentful the poor ghost of a man cut down untimely must be to wander around the edge of this world and attach itself to a living host. When I perform a Great Rite or a rite of banishment and part a ghost from his host and send it to the otherworld the host regains life and the ghost is also freed. It is good to save one on the verge of death but is it not a thankful and marvellous thing to open the way for a ghost that gropes about having lost its way, and let it fly across to the otherworld? I cannot count the number

140

of people I have saved nor the number of ghosts I have sent to the otherworld. Whenever I do that I see clearly with my own eyes. I see clearly the ghost that comes out of a man and goes to the otherworld. Go and ask other people if there ever was anyone who was not rid of their ghost by my rite of banishment. Ask also if there was ever any ghost that was not ferried across to the otherworld by my Great Rite. So what evil thing do you accuse me of having done? What is it that makes your mother turn your stomach so? However well I think of your man Jesus I can see him as no more than we, spirit children. So why must you revere a long-dead spirit child from a distant foreign land and turn away from our own land's living spirit child?'

'Mother if you insult our Lord any more I shall leave this house.'

Yongsul jumped to his feet in a rage. Shocked, Eulhwa clutched at his clothes. Tears were even glistening in her eyes.

'Sul, my son, must even you also despise me? Why is it that you cannot try to understand my words?'

'Mother!' Yongsul's voice was also choked with sudden grief.

'Please don't worry, I shall never betray you or Wolhie.'

'Thank you my son. Then let me ask you one more thing. Where did you sleep last night?' Still sitting down, Eulhwa looked at Yongsul full in the face. As if he had already planned this out Yongsul answered in the low and modest Seoul speech.

'I slept in the chestnut tree village at Father's.'

'My son, precious as a thousand pieces of gold, why did you have to go when I told you not to?'

'Mother, please don't be upset in the least. Is it not meet and fitting to acknowledge one's father? But, mother, I shall remain your son forever.'

Yongsul spoke in the soft local speech. Slowly he opened the door and went out. Eulhwa sat and looked listlessly at the door through which her son had gone for a long time.

'Oh, I am losing my precious son, precious as a thousand pieces of gold because of that bloody Jesus devil.'

All alone she gnashed her teeth.

Chapter Fifteen
BIBLE AND KNIFE

That day when Yongsul returned to his father Yongsul resolved not to see his mother for at least a week. Not only did his mother's harsh and insulting words about God still rankle but more than that he wished to give her the opportunity to repent of her words. But he could not spend several days in this fashion with no clear purpose at his father's. There, he resolved to his foster-father at Kampo which he had been planning to do for a long time.

For some reason Bangdol recognized him immediately and welcomed him saying:

'Well if it is not Yongsul? What brings you here? My, how you have grown!'

That night, sitting facing each other in front of a table loaded with sliced raw fish and steamed rice-cakes, they told each other of what had passed. When Yongsul brought out the news that he had been to see his father, Bangdol at once said:

'That's very good. Your mother won't be able to live together with anyone except for my Wolhie.' A little later he added, 'As a person your mother is kind, generous with her help and infinitely good, but since she is possessed by a spirit she differs from ordinary people. However hard you try to understand each other you will find it hard to get on with each other.'

When Yongsul left the next day his foster-father went with

him as far as the foot of the pass and said, holding Yongsul's hands.

'I will also drop in some time, then I can also see my Wolhie . . .'

The day after he returned from Kampo was a Sunday so he went to attend chapel and met Elder Park at the church. He could not but relate what had happened. When Elder Park heard everything he shook his head and told him off.

'That is not like you at all. If, as you said to me you are resolved to spread God's word, never lose heart no matter what happens. Then you must ignore whatever the other person says and steadfastly do what you must do. If you act angrily, stung by that person's abuse, then will that not provoke and enrage that person?'

'As you say, respected Elder, it seems that I have acted without much thought. When this evening's worship is ended I shall go back to my mother's and give her my apology.' Yongsul truthfully admitted his mistake.

That night even after the end of evening worship Yongsul stayed behind and prayed in the empty chapel. He prayed that through God's boundless love that his mother's sins be forgiven and that he make her into a woman who knew how to revere God. Hot tears splashed down from his eyes. After he had finished praying he wiped his eyes for a long time and left the church.

The alley in front of the church was pitch dark and countless stars were twinkling above his head.

'If all these stars were God's eyes he would see right into my mind,' thought Yongsul as he walked slowly along the dark alley.

When the alley was about to join the main road he lifted his head again. At that instant it seemed that the stars had all turned into Wolhie's eyes, looking down at him.

'Elder brother, how could you not come home for four whole days?' whispered Wolhie's eyes as they looked reproachfully down at him.

'Yes, forgive me Dalhie. As Elder Park said I have been narrow-minded. In future I shall not forsake you.'

Promising this to Wolhie in his mind he walked along the bend of the stream. As he came to the alley which led to his house the road seemed to get darker and the stars came crashing down on his forehead as if a stone wall had come crashing down. When he raised his head his footsteps had led him to the foot of the stone wall that ran about the house. Just as he thought he saw a faint light shining above the thick weeds in the garden he noticed an opaque paper lantern hanging from the eaves.

'Is she offering some sort of sacrifice to the spirits?' he thought to himself. Whenever Eulhwa went out to perform a rite or do a sacrifice or a ceremony beseeching the spirits she was wont to hang such an opaque white paper lantern on the eaves.

Wading through the weeds and reaching the stone step he heard from the kitchen a muttering sound as if someone was reciting a spell. When he walked up to the front of the step he realized that this was his mother's voice and that it streamed out together with a faint light from the kitchen.

Out of curiosity he went in front of the kitchen and looked inside. At that instant he felt his chest heave with an indescribable feeling of shock and revulsion. The whole kitchen was plastered with bits of coloured paper and strips of cloth so that it looked as if someone had moved a spirit shrine to the kitchen. On each of the two fireplaces that lay at each side a lamp made by dipping wicks in a saucerful of clarified rapeseed oil was burning. On the upper wall where the cauldron was hanging there was a large picture of the 'Divine General' dressed in green and brown, brandishing a long spear high in the air and trampling with his big feet on a demon with scarlet clothes and scarlet face. Above it there was a little picture inscribed 'Great Spirit of the Holy Mother of the Celestial peach' who was her titulary spirit, and on either side of the Divine General there were pasted up half hazardly countless pictures in vivid colour of demons or ghosts. There was a small window set into the wall above the fireplace on the right and above this window was pasted the picture of the crimson demon that Wolhie had been painting the other day. On the main beam as well as the wall there hung countless lengths of thread and attached to each thread were bits of coloured paper and rags and all sorts of pictures so that it was hard to tell whether one was going up to heaven or down to hell.

On each fireplace lit by the saucer lamp there was a little

table. The table in the right held a bowl of sacrificial rice, a bowl of cold water, a dish of salt and a small plate full of yellow and green bean sprouts, blue-bell roots, bracken and courgette. The table on the left held in the middle a rattle and a pair of cymbals and to one side a carving knife.

It was impossible to know what each of those things meant, but from the fact that his mother had called the crimson demon that Wolhie had drawn a Jesus devil, and the air of disorderly preparations it was easy to guess that the underlying purpose was to persecute and eliminate the Christian religion in which Yongsul believed.

Yongsul's heart pounded and he felt dizzy. In the heat of anger he wished to open the door and leap inside to overturn everything that had been laid out in such disorder: pictures, strips of cloth and offerings. But he could do nothing but contain his rage, since if he had done such a thing not only would he not be able to see his mother again but he would destroy all his mother's chances to repent.

Neither could he run away from home for he was prevented from doing so by the thought of Elder Park's words: '. . . that is not like you at all . . . If you are resolved to spread God's word you must ignore whatever the other person says and steadfastly do what you must do . . .'

Knees trembling, he was just about to turn back when his mother, who until now had been kneeling in front of the makeshift altar rubbing her palms together and reciting some sort of incantation, straightened herself and picked up the rattle from the table on the left. She immediately started to sing in a high pitched voice.

'In the sky, the Great Sky God
Under the earth the Great God of the Underground,
The Mountain God in the mountains
The Dragon God in the water.
Hither I go, all belongs to the Great Spirit
Thither I go, all belongs to the Great Spirit
From when our hair turns black
Our life, to be born, to die, to live
All is under the Shade of the Great Spirit.
My Yongsul
Twenty-one this year

Like gold, like silver
Like jade on a diadem.
The three Gods of Birth
Gave you life
The God of the Big Dipper
Gave you longevity
The God of the Hearth
Gave you luck
The God of the Kitchen
Gave you plenty.
Our Yongsul,
A star in the sky
A pearl in the sea
My Yongsul
All the people in the world
Cherish you
Praise you
Revere you
My Yongsul
Since the three Gods of Birth
Look after you
The God of the Big Dipper
Helps you
The Spirit of the ancestors
Guard you
So Jesus Devil
I cast you out!'

Yelling at the top of her voice, she went to the fireplace on
the left and picked up the knife on the table. She aimed the
knife several times at the crimson image of the demon on the
wall that faced her and began to sing again shaking her rattle.

'With knife in one hand
And fire in the other
I cast out the red demon
I scatter it to a place
Far far away
Fire demon, be off!
You hungry demon
From the farthest reaches of the West

Who stands in way of others
Who drags down to oblivion
My precious Child.
You fire demon,
Ghost of a long-dead bachelor
You should be struck by lightning
Be off in a trice!
If you stay and do not go
I shall tie you up with white horse leather
In a window blind of thorny ash
So tight that you cannot move,
And send you off to deepest Hell.
Jesus devil is burning bright
Fire demon is consumed by fire
When the demon is all burnt up
My son sits like a taoist immortal
And comes to see the three Gods of Birth
And comes to see his mother.'

Shaking the knife and rattle Eulhwa started to dance. Whenever she stared at the wall in front of her, her eyes turned in their sockets so that the whites of her eyes which one could not usually see were revealed. There was murder in her eyes. Yongsul thought that his mother was most definitely not herself but had become another person. It was clear from the way only the whites of her eyes showed.

His teeth chattered from rage and fear. He walked to the stepping stone and collapsed on the threshold. Staring at the heavens like one gone mad he regained his breath and walked towards the weeds. He suppressed the desire to wade past them and walk in and knelt in front of the weeds and started to pray. Again and again he repeated the phrase. 'Our father who art in heaven.' He felt calmer.

After praying he stood for a long time in front of the black and tangled weeds and entered the room. When she saw Yongsul, Wolhie, who had been sitting next to the window which looked into the kitchen and had been listening to her mother's complaints, jumped up with joy upon seeing her brother. She clasped her arms around his shoulders and clung to his breast.

'Brother, brother, why not come? For four days . . . .'

147

And she lifted up four of her slender white fingers.

'I'm sorry, Wolhie.'

Holding her hands he sat down on the colder part of the heated floor. Wolhie looked at him for long time and questioned him again.

'Brother, tell me. Why never come, where did you sleep?'

He did not wish to avoid answering her but since he could not give her a complicated explanation he just said:

'I was at Father's.'

'Where? There?' asked Wolhie pointing to the east.

To her, 'father' just meant Sung Bangdol at Kampo. Yongsul also had known no other father until he had left for Kirim Temple. Yongsul was at a loss for words. True, he had been to Kampo, but he had meant Lee Sungchool of the chestnut tree village.

'I have also been to see that father but . . .' Yongsul broke off in mid-sentence.

Not understanding him very well she said:

'Mother a-a-a-ngry.'

'Since when?'

Wolhie said nothing and just raised three of her fingers.

'Since three days ago?'

Wolhie nodded and continued.

'Mother, not ever eat. For three nights just do those rites.' She raised three of her fingers again.

Yongsul took this as meaning that for three nights since he had left for chestnut tree village for the second time she had eaten almost nothing, carrying on in the kitchen.

'Wolhie, you want to see East Coast father, don't you?'

'Yes, as much as this.' She spread open her arms to show how much.

'He also says he wants to see you.'

'Me too.'

'Go and stay with Father (at Kampo). You would like that, wouldn't you?'

He asked this because more than anything else he wished to take her away from his mother. But Wolhie shook her head from side to side and pointing to the kitchen, said:

'Mother get a. .a. .angry.'

'But mother will still have me.'

'For four days brother don't come. Mother a. .a. .angry.'

148

It seemed that Wolhie believed that she must not leave mother. But he could not persuade her otherwise with just a few words. Yongsul knelt and teaching his sister to do likewise, took out a bible from his breast. As he was in the habit of doing at his evening prayers he opened it at random and started reading.

'And he came out, and went, as he was wont, to the mount of olives; and his disciples followed him. And when he was at that place, he said unto them, Pray that ye enter not into temptation. And he was withdrawn from them about a stone's cast, and kneeled down, and prayed, saying, Father, if thou be willing, remove this cup from me: nevertheless not my will, but thine, be done. And there appeared an angel unto him from heaven, strengthening him. And being in an agony, he prayed more earnestly: and his sweat was as if it were great drops of Blood falling down to the ground . . .'

Yongsul read up to here and then closed the bible.

'Let us pray.' He said.

Closing her eyes, Wolhie followed Yongsul and bowed her head.

'Our God the Father, I beseech thee to save our pitiful family. My mother is possessed of a shaman spirit and knoweth not how foolish and sinful her actions are. I beseech thee to save my pitiful mother and younger sister from the pit of infamy. Lord, I believe that when thou father hast sent this weak and foolish lamb to this pit of infamy thou didst so with the intention of saving us. Grant unto this weak and foolish lamb the strength and wisdom to do thy will. If it be to save my mother and sister from this pit of infamy I shall not falter, Lord but go through fire and water to save them. Lord I beseech thee take pity on us . . .'

When he had gone thus far he heard the sound of the door opening and shutting. Eulhwa seemed to be coming in. He silently finished his prayer, slowly opened his eyes and half straightening his crooked back greeted his mother.

'Mother, I have come back.'

As if she was utterly weary Eulhwa just looked at Wolhie and Yongsul, her arms hanging down at her side and plonked herself down. She seized Yongsul's wrist and sighed.

'Please forgive me, mother. I am sorry to have caused you so much worry.'

149

'My son, why do you try to avoid me?'

Her voice was hoarse like one who had cried for many days.

'Mother, wherever I am my heart is always with you. I shall always be your son.'

'How nice if that were true. I wake up in the middle of the night only to find that you are not there. I could not bear to live for grief and anger.'

'Mother, please don't worry, your son shall go nowhere.'

'Thank you my son.'

Wiping her eyes she rose and spread his bedding on the cooler part of the floor. As always Eulhwa slept in the middle and Wolhie slept on the warmer part of the floor. Sleeping on the same floor as they did, they more or less fell asleep at the same time. Since he had left chestnut tree village at dawn and spent all day giving worship at the chapel, and since he had also spent a long time at home as well, when he put head to pillow he was very tired. He fell into a deep sleep for some four hours.

Around dawn, when a cold wind swept into the room, Yongsul, though he was still half asleep, felt somehow empty. He opened his eyes and felt immediately that something was missing from his chest. His hand went instinctively to his chest. The bible that he kept next his breast had disappeared. He jumped to his feet.

His mother who had been lying in the middle was not to be seen. Wolhie was fast asleep facing the wall. As he took in the scene in the room he heard from the kitchen sounds of incantation that he had heard last night. He felt instinctively that it was his mother's doing which had made his bible disappear. At that moment not knowing what to do he clenched both his fists and his whole body shook in a tremor. At the same time in the kitchen the mumbling incantation grew to a screaming complaint.

Unbeknownst to himself Yongsul kicked open the door and ran out shoeless from the stone step to the kitchen. But the kitchen doors had been bolted, fastened with a beam so that he could not get in. There was a largish chink between the two doors through which he could see clearly into the kitchen. As in the night before Eulhwa was holding a rattle in her left hand and a knife in the right. The moment he had pushed at the doors her voice rose to a sudden crescendo.

'Jesus demon is retreating
Putting shoes on
At the Spirit's holy mountain
Wrapping feet in cloth of cotton
At the tomb of the God of War
Attaching bells to both his ears
Walks in time to the sounding bells
Jingle jangle jingle jangle
How he doth go quickly walking
Over pass and across the stream.
If you go now when we see you?
He cannot come for aching feet
Though you wish to come in springtime
Yet you are too weak from hunger
To try and make the journey back.'

Eulhwa jangled the rattle and pretended to strike over and over again at the kitchen door. Here eyes turned up in their sockets, and the whites of her eyes showed even more clearly. Though his skin crawled at the sight of her Yongsul could not bear to leave his bible in her hands. He put his hand through the chink and shook the door with all his might, then gave it a swift kick. A hinge gave way and the bolt dropped to the ground so that the door gaped on its hinges and opened askew. He leapt into the kitchen and shouted at the top of his voice.

'Mother! What have you done with my bible?'

Eulhwa on her part started to shout at the top of her voice.

'Demon, be off! Away with you!
Fire demon who begged in the far Western Reaches
If you don't go and I catch you
I shall tie you up with white horse leather
In a window blind of thorny ash
And roast you in an iron cauldron.'

But Yongsul was already deaf to everything for his bible was spouting forth blue sparks from the fireplace on the right.

The book seemed to have been burning for quite a while for the corners were already charred to a blackish cinder and the red flame was dancing from the centre to the spine giving off a bluish smoke.

Yongsul tried first of all to put out the fire on his bible.

The bowl of water lay on the tray on the fireplace on the right but Eulhwa blocked his way, the whites of her eyes showing. Screaming at the top of her voice she brandished the kitchen knife.

'Be off with you, fire devil!

Be off with you, Jesus devil!'

But Yongsul's eyes were blind to everything, nor did anything scare him. As he ran to the fireplace on the right and tried to pick up his bible he felt a searing pain in his chest. But he dropped his hard-won bible on the cauldron lid, for what he held in his hands was no longer bible but a ball of fire and he knew not whether it was his hand or his chest that felt hot. The knife still sticking in his left breast crimson blood started to stain his clothes. Below the fireplace Eulhwa hugged her son's body to her.

Chapter Sixteen
THE PAPER LANTERN

It was the very same evening. When Sung Bangdol came from the East Coast with dried seaweed and kelp and dried salted yellow coaker and other seafoods wrapped up in a cloth to see Yongsul and Wolhie, Yongsul lay like one dead on the cooler part of the 'ondol' floor. He was still bleeding. The whole of his chest was a crimson lump of dried blood, but one could tell by the spot where the knife had torn through the fabric that the wound was on the left.

'Yongsul, what has happened? Yongsul!'

'Father.' Yongsul spoke in a low voice, so faint that it could hardly be heard.

'Yes, Yongsul, what has happened here?'

Yongsul lay silent for a long time and opened his eyes after a long time.

'Elder Park . . . please get me Elder Park.'

Realizing that Yongsul was near death Sung Bangdol ran out of the house to look for Elder Park's. When Elder Park heard of Yongsul's state from Sung Bangdol he asked with a look of shock on his face.

'What? His mother does such a deed?'

'It seems his mother has lost her reason.'

'Then we cannot leave him there. Let us go.'

And they set off even taking some hired men with them.

When she saw Yongsul being carried out on a stretcher, Eulhwa who had been praying and rubbing her hands together in the kitchen ran out shouting:

153

'Who is it? Who is stealing my son?'

When Bangdol tried to block her by opening his arms she pushed him aside and thundered at Elder Park.

'What are you doing? Are you also Jesus devils? What do you hold against me that you try to take away my son?'

Elder Park stamped his feet and shouted in answer.

'Wretch! Will you not be content until you devour your own child?'

Then Eulhwa laughed bitterly and said:

'Oh, how awful! Do Jesus devils devour their own children?'

'You false and cunning creature!' Thundered Elder Park and turned around.

The stretcher was already going out of sight past the stone wall. Eulhwa wailed in a voice to crack her throat.

'Jesus devils are taking my son away!' She collapsed in a heap on top of the weeds as if she had lost her breath while shouting.

Early next morning as Yongsul called his mother for the last time before death Bangdol ran out of Elder Park's. Eulhwa and Wolhie followed him to Elder Park's. Entering the room where her son lay Eulhwa shouted:

'My son, Yongsul, what has happened?' At Eulhwa's tearful voice he slowly opened his eyes. He seemed to recognize her. A little later his gaze turned to Wolhie.

'Mother, please forgive me.' His voice crept in his throat and could barely be heard. 'I go to heaven before you. Mother, Wolhie, let us meet in heaven.' He barely managed to utter these words before he closed his eyes.

'Sul, my son, why do you die before me? No you shall not die. For what crime should you die? You have committed no crime. If I can drive out the fire demon in you you shall come running with arms outstretched to your mother. Even this very instant I shall drive out the fire demon in you, so bear with me a while.' When she had gone this far she suddenly shot out one of her arms over her son's face and, her eyes turning up in their sockets so that only the whites showed, said: 'Do you understand, my Sul?' She screamed her throat rip.

Bangdol and the neighbours who had been beside her then dragged her out. And as she was being taken out, she resisted with all her might and shouted.

'Who are you? What do you hold against me that you steal my son and try to kill him?'

As Eulhwa and Wolhie left Yongsul's father Lee Sungchool and his grandmother opened the sliding paper door which led to the room and entered.

Eyes closed Yongsul lay as one dead. And Sungchool took Yongsul's lifeless wrist by his hand and sobbed loudly.

'Oh, you fool, you fool! What crime did I commit? Had I known this would happen I would not have looked for you.'

Grandmother wiped once more her red and swollen eyes, saying:

'God is cruel, God is cruel. Why did he not call this old body instead of yours? Since last night your mother has not eaten a thing and has been praying, praying the whole while.'

When she was complaining thus to herself Elder Park entered the room. He sat quietly next to Lee Sungchool. He closed his eyes and prayed in silence for a long time, then put his hand under Yongsul's nostrils to see if he still breathed and said in a low voice.

'Master Lee.'

There was silence. Again he called out.

'Master Lee.'

Silence.

'Yongsul.'

Thus did he call out three times. At last as if he had regained consciousness Yongsul slowly slit his eyes open.

'Reverend Elder Park.'

Elder Park took his hand and said:

'Master Lee, look at me. Your father and grandmother are all here.'

But Yongsul closed his eyes again as if he could not hear Elder Park. After a long while Yongsul opened his eyes and said:

'Our Lord in heaven, please take this poor soul. And please save my poor mother.'

Scarcely had he said this when he died. Tears had gathered in his closed eyes.

Three days later Yongsul's body was buried in a public cemetery after a quiet church funeral.

Bangdol was far gone with drink when he came back from the funeral. Though he did not usually drink, as a funeral was a funeral he found it hard to bear it cold sober. Still wearing his shoes he jumped onto the threshold and pulled fiercely at the door. But Eulhwa was not in the room and Wolhie sat alone weeping.

'Where is mother?' His voice was rough as it never had been before.

'Granny Po . . .' answered Wolhie as she sat and wiped her tears.

'Did Granny Pox drop in?'

Wolhie nodded silently.

'Did mother leave with Granny Pox?'

Silent, Wolhie neither nodded nor shook her head. It seemed that she had seen Granny Pox drop in but had not seen the two of them leave.

'But why should old Pox come here? So old it must have been a hard walk for her. Did she hear of the stabbing and come? Did she take Eulhwa with her?' thought Bangdol. But he had no need to know where she had gone nor with whom she had left. Had she been there he could have given her a good cursing but who knew it was probably better that she was absent.

'Wolhie, come out.'

'Why, father?'

'Hurry on out!'

Without further askance Wolhie got up and came out to the threshold. Bangdol took her by the wrist and left the house. There was a donkey standing just outside the stone wall. Bangdol carried Wolhie and sat her on the donkey. The groom who had been crouching by the wall then got up and took the donkey's halter.

'Let's go.'

'Where, father?'

'If you stay here you shall end up like your brother. Come with me.'

'And mother?'

At first Bangdol did not answer Wolhie's question. After a long while he looked at her and said:

'Mother will know too.'

That night also, there was an opaque paper lantern hanging alight from the eaves of Eulhwa's house, as it had the night before.

156